# FOOD F      DS

# FOOD FOR FRIENDS

**Sophie Grigson**

EBURY PRESS
LONDON

For Jane and Geoffrey

First published in 1987

This edition published in 1995 by
Ebury Press, Random House, 20 Vauxhall Bridge Road,
London SW1V 2SA

1 3 5 7 9 10 8 6 4 2

Text copyright © Sophie Grigson 1987 and 1995

Sophie Grigson has asserted her right under the Copyright, Designs and
Patents Act, 1988, to be identified as the author of this work.

Random House Australia Pty Limited, 20 Alfred Street, Milsons Point,
Sydney, New South Wales 2061, Australia

Random House New Zealand Limited, 18 Poland Road, Glenfield,
Auckland 10, New Zealand

Random House South Africa Pty Limited, PO Box 337, Bergvlei,
South Africa

Random House UK Limited Reg. No. 95400

A CIP catalogue record for this book is available from the British Library.

ISBN 0 09180888 X

Designed by The Senate and Bob Vickers

Printed and bound in Great Britain by
Mackays of Chatham plc, Kent

Sophie Grigson was born in Wiltshire and educated partly in England and partly in France. Her many previous books include *Sophie Grigson's Ingredients Book* and *Sophie's Table*, along with the books which accompanied her highly successful television series – *Eat Your Greens/Grow Your Greens*, *Travels à la Carte* and *Sophie's Meat Course*. She has written for many national magazines and newspapers, including the *Evening Standard*, *The Independent* and the *Sunday Times*, for which she currently writes a regular cookery feature. Sophie Grigson has two children and lives in Northamptonshire.

# CONTENTS

# INTRODUCTION

I began to write about food quite by chance. My father would have disagreed with me on that point. Or at least, he would have said that it was inevitable that I would write about something, and that the break, the beginning, would come sooner or later. He always held that all four of his children would end up as writers of one sort or another, and he was right. My two half-sisters and my half-brother all write about their own specialist fields. And now I'm throwing in my two ha'porth as well.

Nature or nurture? Certainly the latter, and possibly both. Who knows? Every room in our farmhouse (with the exception of the bathroom, the downstairs loo and the larder) was lined with books. There were always higgledy-piggledy piles of new and old review copies on the wooden settle in the hall. In the spare room, the natural history books; on the upstairs landing one could find all of Shakespeare, Jim Pennythorne Hughes' book on surnames (a great favourite of mine as a child), next door to that a dictionary of English placenames and their origins. Pevsner's architectural guides to England, amongst others. Novels lived in the sitting room. Poetry and reference in my father's study; art in the library and of course, children's books in my room.

As my mother's interest in cooking grew, and her career as a cookery writer took off, her collection of cookery books became too large for the kitchen, and began to fill her study.

They both worked from home. My father would be completely absorbed in his writing from morning to evening. It was hell trying to get him to emerge from his cubbyhole for meals. But when he did, he was an enthusiastic critic of my mother's cooking. Meal times were important, whether it was just the three of us, or whether there were other members of the family, or friends around the table as well. The talk was often of literature, art or food, but not in a pompous, or pretentious way. Good books, good paintings, good food; these things all enhance the quality of life.

## Memories of France   When I was about two years old, we stayed for the first time in a small French village called Trôo, in the valley of the Loir (without an 'e' — it's a tributary of the big one with an 'e'). It was once a stone-quarrying village, then weavers moved into the man-made caves, setting up huge looms that stretched from one side of the cave to the other. In some, one can still see the hollows cut into the rock to support the wooden cross-bars, and woad, the plant from which the blue dyes were extracted, grows wild on the hillside. It is now a very beautiful, but crumbling, troglodyte village. Too many caves have been abandoned.

There are some houses, clustered around the main road at the foot of the hill, and around the church on top of the hill, and some caves have had a room or false façade added on in front. After several visits to the village, my mother bought one of these. Tiny, without electricity or running water, but with a view that stretches out across the river, over the frescoed church of St. Jacques, and right across the valley to the hills on the far side.

From then on we spent three or four months a year there. I quickly learnt French (it was either that or have no friends to play with – not much of a choice when you are three or four years old), went to school there, fetched the bread or croissants in the mornings, and soon found out that food was of immense importance to every Jean, Pierre and François in the village. My best friends (one the daughter of a gardener, the other the son of a road mender) and I played endless games of restaurants, and *pâtisseries*, concocting glorious confections out of mud, chalk and water.

And it was in Trôo that the idea of my mother's first cookery book, *Charcuterie*, was born. Soon she was writing and cooking full-time, and so I learnt, as it were, at her knee. In England, people naturally congregated in the large kitchen, sitting and chatting over a cup of coffee, or as my mother prepared the meal. Naturally, I spent much of my time in there too, helping when I could. Later on, she would leave me there alone, armed with recipe book, ingredients and utensils, as she withdrew to her room. If I needed help, or disaster struck, she was nearby, but she never interfered, never grabbed the knife saying 'No, no, this is how you are meant to do it'. Heaven knows whether what I turned out was edible, but it gave me confidence and independence in the kitchen.

In France, the kitchen was a great deal smaller. In fact it was a converted fireplace, with two gas rings and a grill. I think my mother rather enjoyed this. It meant she couldn't be expected to produce an elaborate meal. But the meals that did emerge from the fireplace were, nonetheless, marvellous. Simple, but with a flair and imagination that turned the basic ingredients into a feast. It is true that in France, the raw and prepared foods that one can buy, even in a small village, are so superior to their English equivalents, that one hardly needs to cook. Why should the French housewife bother making a pudding, say, when every baker in town is baking fresh fruit tarts daily, when the *pâtissier* sells all kinds of chocolatey or creamy little cakes, when the local fruit is sweet and ripe and plentiful?

So in France I discovered the joys of shopping in a country that adores food, and discusses it with passion. I discovered that with good ingredients, the simplest of meals can be turned into something special. In England I learnt about the pleasures of cooking. And I soon realised that a good meal is more than a series of dishes placed upon a table. Convivial, relaxing company is every bit as important. What fun is there in constantly worrying whether the next course will be all right, or in spending the entire meal bent double over a hot stove, whilst others eat your magnificent creations without you?

So, with all that as a background, it is not so surprising that my father was convinced that I would end up putting pen to paper. Nor is it surprising that I write about food. But until a couple of months ago it was a sideline, on top of a full-time job. Whatever I've been doing though, I've always cooked, for myself and for friends. As a student in Manchester, I learnt to cook on a tight budget. I did eat baked beans sometimes. I still do. I like them. But I was fascinated by the West Indian food shops, and the Indian sweetshops and curry houses.

**Discovering Italy** When I was nineteen, I made another major discovery. Italy. I've returned every year since, with only one exception, and that hurt. I fell in love, if not at first sight, at least within a couple of days. My first taste was of Naples, Pompeii, then Sicily, followed by quick dips at Florence and Venice. Since then I've seen much more of Italy. Rome, with its horrendous traffic, strange ruins, decaying palaces, all its noise and life and vitality, is the city I was meant to be born in, but Siena is the jewel.

To the horror of many northern Italians, I have a passion for the South. Sicily, desired and conquered and embellished by so many great Empires over the course of its history, was my first experience of southern Italy (though no self-respecting Sicilian would care to be called an Italian). Siracusa, Agrigento, the valley of the seven temples, sloping down towards the sea, amidst clouds of almond blossom. But the dry, brown, parched landscape of the interior was what touched me most. That and the kindness and generosity of every Sicilian.

The southern food is simple. The North may have more sophisticated restaurants, but when it comes down to the lower end of the market, the cheap little *trattorie*, southern ones win outright.

More recently, I spent four days in one small town, in Calabria, the toe of Italy. The great speciality in Tropea is the sweet red onion (and I've never tasted better). The onion pizzas, cooked in an 18th century wood oven were easily amongst the best I've ever eaten. The tomato sauces of every eating-place in town were flavoured with the rich caramel of sun-dried tomatoes. Old women sold jars and strings of dried aubergines, and tomatoes, and bunches of herbs, or slices of *nduja* – a thick paste-like sausage made of pork and chilli peppers and salt. Huge jars of salted capers, and a chilli-cured ham that we devoured every lunch-time. The fish we ate in the evening had been caught early that morning.

The food there in Tropea, and throughout the South is honest, fresh and unadulterated, or preserved by the most elementary of methods. Sun-ripened fruit, and herbs and vegetables have an intensity of flavour that comes as a revelation. The poverty of the South has prevented the development of a sophisticated culinary tradition. But to the foreign visitor this is of no consequence. Why play around with things that are so delicious to begin with?

My visits to Italy have inevitably influenced the way I cook. I'm lucky that the nearest shop to my flat is a small Italian grocery. The smell of cheeses, salamis and hams envelops you as you walk in. It's like all those little dark Italian *alimentari*, where I've bought *panini* (filled rolls) and a bottle of mineral water for a picnic lunch, in the shade of a piece of ancient masonry. Over here, a quarter of salami or prosciutto, a mozzarella, some tomatoes from a nearby vegetable stall, and I can put together a delicious lunch in minutes. The tomato won't be up to Italian standards – it will need a pinch of sugar, and a dash of vinegar, as well as salt and olive oil and basil – but this still seems to me to be a perfect light lunch.

I like to cook for myself, but like most people, I prefer to cook for friends. Sharing a meal, talking, and laughing over good food and wine, around a comfortable table, or even balancing plates on your knee, is such a pleasure. The food is important, but not everything. If, like me, you do not have the time to spend the whole day in the kitchen, if you're working, then the last thing you're going to want is to have to fuss, and rush, and spend most of the evening in the kitchen perfecting some grand dish, that will, after all, be consumed within a few minutes.

## Adaptable planning

The tricky thing is to balance the desire to create something wonderful, with the desire to spend time with your guests. Adaptable planning and imagination are the keys. By adaptable planning, I mean that you should start off with a rough idea of what you want to cook, and then let it change as circumstance dictates. Many dishes can be prepared or cooked the night before (e.g. the *Orange Jellies*, or *Apple and Pistachio Mousse*, or the duck for the *Devilled Duck Salad*), but that is precious little consolation if you didn't think ahead at all.

Say you wanted to try out the recipe for *Fichi Ripieni*, and as you shop in your brief lunch hour, the only fig you can find is the one being mauled by a starving pigeon. Either you scour every shop within a five-mile radius which you can't do, because you've only got an hour to get everything else, or else you change the recipe. You might spot some marvellous, juicy-looking, golden pears – they would be good filled with the ricotta mixture that was meant for the elusive figs, or in that simple *Gratin of Fresh Pears*, or just on their own, or with some really crumbly Lancashire cheese. That is an example of adaptable planning and imagination.

In the second half of the introduction to each chapter, you will find a whole host of suggestions for simple ways to use that particular ingredient. These are dishes that have no strict formulas, that can be improvised and played around with. You must decide on the exact quantities yourself – balance these things to fit in with the rest of your meal, and with what is available. Some of the suggestions may seem obvious, and they should be considered as reminders and more importantly as springboards for your own innovations.

When you see bright, healthy looking fennel in the greengrocers, look at the rest of their produce. Are the tomatoes looking good? Think of fennel in a tomato sauce. Maybe the fishmonger has some red mullet that could be baked on a bed of fennel? Or another kind of fish that could be used instead? Is there an Italian delicatessen nearby, where you could buy a wedge of fresh Parmesan? That's for a gratin, but then again, that fennel would be good with pasta . . . That's the way to use these ideas. They should help to make shopping easier, and more enjoyable. If you are in doubt about quantities, or variations, then talk to your suppliers. In an intelligent shop selling good foods, you will find that the shopkeeper is more than willing to give advice and help. In most supermarkets you lose out in this way, but you'll save on time. It's six of one and half a dozen of the other.

You may notice that there are a large number of fruit-based puddings in this book. There are several reasons for this. Firstly, I like fruit-based puddings. Secondly, they tend to be light and refreshing and a good way to end a meal. And thirdly, perhaps most importantly, they are a great aid to adaptability. If you find, because you had to work late, or because your train was cancelled, or whatever, that you do not have time to prepare the pudding you intended to make, then you can serve the fruit as they are, and no-one will be any the wiser.

Throughout the book, there are examples of possible menus. Personally, I have never once followed a menu laid out in a cookery book, so these ones should not be seen as law, any more than the recipes should be, but as a starting point for any adaptable planning you may be contemplating, and as imagination joggers.

With a couple of exceptions, I've stuck to the three-course formula – starter, main course and pudding (or fruit and cheese). I like that three-tiered structure, but I wouldn't necessarily stick with the traditional definition of each course. Sometimes start and main course will be of roughly similiar proportions, possibly quite interchangeable. Sometimes, if, say, there is a particularly intriguing but rich and filling recipe for a pudding that I have been longing to try, then I'll forget any notions of a first course. I don't want my friends to walk out feeling like over-stuffed sofas, nor do I want my culinary efforts to be wasted.

**Complementary dishes**  If I'm cooking for a large number of people, then I will probably abandon any attempts at formal structure. Several dishes that complement each other, but stand equally well on their own two feet will arrive on the table simultaneously and the guests can make their own choice about what and how much to eat, and in what order.

And if I'm really pushed for time, I will just concentrate on one all-encompassing dish – a huge steaming bowl of *Fish Chowder*, a moist perfumed risotto, a rich gratin of potatoes and smoked salmon. With it, or after it, one or two really good salads – one lively green one (no floppy tasteless leaves, thank you), and perhaps a tomato and olive salad. Lots of good bread, one or two large pieces of farmhouse cheese, followed with fruit, nuts and sweetmeats, and lots of real coffee, and there you are – a most delicious meal, quick to prepare, satisfying to eat, and you barely have to spend any time in the kitchen once you start eating.

If you keep a selection of interesting tinned or preserved items in the store cupboard, then you should be able to put together a varied first course or pudding with ease. There are suggestions for bits and pieces to add to a mixed hors d'oeuvre, or mixed desert, throughout the book. The kind of things I'm talking about might be tinned anchovies, cannellini beans for salads, a tin of foie gras brought back from a trip to France, humus (jazz it up with fruity olive oil, paprika and fresh parsley), dried tomatoes, mushrooms preserved in olive oil, or, on the sweet side, stem ginger in syrup, candied fruits or peel, Indian sugar candy, chocolate brazil nuts, and so on and so forth.

Add a grilled pepper salad, scrambled eggs, hams and charcuterie, quails' eggs, pâté, chutneys and relishes. And at the other end of the meal, fresh fruit – cherries, greengages, clementines, lychees, mangosteens, grapes – fruits that people can eat without knives and forks, toying with a few now and then, as the mood takes them.

Make sure you have lots of freshly-baked bread – the best you can get. If I have the time, I will go to one particular bakery in London's Covent Garden which makes a three-seed bread (poppy, sunflower and linseed) that is heavenly. Otherwise I like a moist granary loaf, a crusty white cottage loaf, or the yellow-crumbed rounds of Moroccan bread that they make just round the corner. Other basic essentials are good butter and a pepper mill filled with whole black peppercorns.

**Instant salad dressings**   I make salad dressings in at least double quantities and keep them in jars in the fridge. If you have two or three different kinds of vinegar (e.g. white wine, tarragon and sherry), and three different oils (olive, grapeseed and walnut maybe), you've got the basis of a wide range of vinaigrettes and mayonnaises, and flavourings for sauces.

Use fresh herbs wherever possible – most supermarkets now stock some fresh herbs throughout the year, and these are usually preferable to dried ones. Where a recipe specifies fresh basil for instance, and there's none to be had, think about using another fresh herb before you reach for the tub of dried hay.

I'm no expert on wines. Like most people I know that white wine goes with white flesh, red with red. But all rules are made to be broken, and wine is there to be enjoyed. In student days it was always *de rigueur* to take a bottle of wine with you to a meal at a friend's house – who could afford to supply both food and drink? Amongst my contemporaries, that habit has stuck, thank heavens, because the costs do mount up quickly. The difference now, though, is that I spend a little more time and money, and pick out a favourite or an untried but recommended wine to take with me. When friends are coming over, I usually have a bottle of nice white chilling in the fridge, and something red, opened and breathing away happily in the kitchen. That seems ample to me.

We need to eat, we need to drink, and we need to breathe. There's little scope for innovation with the last one, but one might as well take pleasure in our other animal necessities. Luckily, the days of cooking to impress, in the home at any rate, seem to be fading fast. No more nervous dinners for the husband's boss, thank you all the same. Only spend hours in the kitchen, preparing something terribly grand, because you enjoy being there. Do it for the oohs and aahs of admiration when you take the finished dish to the table, do it because you want to share something special with people you love, but never because you feel you ought to. If you cook grudgingly, it shows.

This book is about enjoyment – enjoying shopping, enjoying cooking, enjoying sharing food and eating it. Though the emphasis is on entertaining, in most instances the quantities can easily be reduced, to make a supper dish for one or two. I write primarily for myself – this is the kind of book I enjoy reading and using. I've got my fingers crossed in the hope that others will enjoy it too. I'd like to think that some of the ideas and suggestions gathered together here, could make an evening at home, with or without friends, that much more of a treat.

*All recipes are for 6 servings, unless otherwise stated.*

Sophie Grigson, London 1987

Pasta – cheap and cheerful and a thousand and one different ways to serve it. I lived on it when I was younger and travelling around Italy on tuppence ha'penny, and when I came back home to student life. I'm still a fan, cooking pasta for myself, for friends, often in preference to heavier meat dishes.

In Italy, pasta fulfils the same function as Yorkshire pudding does in Yorkshire – its bulk is meant to fill the stomach, so that a small amount of expensive meat can then be made to stretch round the whole family. Outside Italy, we've taken to pasta with gusto. By and large, we've abandoned the en suite meat course, and made pasta the focal point of the meal.

But if one is to serve anything with pasta, it must be a good green salad, or at a pinch a tomato salad. Alternatively, start with a vegetabley first course, follow with pasta, and then serve a salad. I've not included any recipes for the army of tomato-based pasta sauces in this chapter, but a basic tomato sauce (see page 125) can be played around with in all kinds of ways. Add cream to a smooth liquidised sauce, for instance, or add crumbled dried red chillies for a fiery version. Peas, crisply-fried bacon, courgettes, aubergines, olives, cooked mussels, asparagus, sweet peppers, all make good additions. Serve on cooked pasta, or layer with a cheesy sauce and lasagne.

I'm very partial to the really simple ways of serving pasta. Tagliatelle tossed with butter, parsley and lots of Parmesan is lovely, as long as the Parmesan is freshly grated. Forget about those tubs of sawdust. They are a terrible waste of money. Buy a whole piece of Parmesan, and keep it wrapped in foil in the fridge, or buy it grated from a shop where they grate it themselves, every day.

**Flavourings for pasta** Pasta goes well with pepper; crush a couple of spoonfuls of whole peppercorns (just black, or black and green) roughly in a pestle and mortar, and stir into cooked pasta with lots of butter. Serve with Parmesan. Garlic is an obvious addition – infuse one or two cloves of finely-chopped garlic in hot olive oil for a few minutes, strain through a fine sieve if you're not keen on whole lumps of garlic, and stir into pasta with lots of parsley, or other herbs. A crumbled red chilli infused with the garlic will add heat. If you should happen to see fresh truffles for sale, buy one and grate it over hot buttery pasta. Add some chopped parsley, and you will have one of the world's most exquisite dishes.

For a large number of people, serve two or three different coloured pasta – plain white, green spinach and orange tomato – in separate mounds, with bowls of contrasting sauces. Maybe one of the tomato sauces, the cream, mint and lemon sauce in this chapter, and one made with chopped spinach, garlic and orange juice or cream. It takes a bit of juggling with saucepans – prepare the sauces in advance, slightly undercook the pasta, add a knob of butter to each and keep warm in the oven while you reheat the sauces.

Fresh pasta versus dried pasta – well, best of all is going to be your own home-made pasta, but that's not always feasible. Bought fresh pasta has a different texture to dried, and is much quicker to cook. Packaged dried pasta is a good convenience food, that will wait patiently at the back of a cupboard until you need to use it. If you can buy fresh pasta, do. Save the dried for unexpected guests.

Allow 75–100g (3–4 oz) pasta per person, less if you are serving it as a first course. My favourite is tagliatelle, or taglierini (very narrow strips) and so they are the kind I use most. In Italy, there are strict rules about which of the hundreds of different shapes of pasta should be used for which dishes. There are usually good reasons for these rules, but as our choice is more limited, just use whatever most appeals to you.

## Pasta with Cheese and Walnuts

One thing I enjoy about this dish is the way the mozzarella pulls out into long thin threads as you serve it. Great fun as long as you are not intent on being terribly formal and polite. Another pleasing thing is that it makes an almost instant main course – in all, using fresh pasta, it should take about five minutes, once the water has boiled.

Instead of walnuts, you could use bacon, or *pancetta*, cut into strips, or dried porcini – see page 111 for preparation.

SUGGESTED MENU

*Devilled Duck Salad*
*Fusilli with Cheese and Walnuts*
*Red Fruit Gratin*

275 g (10 oz) Gorgonzola
2 mozzarellas, weighing about 175 g (6 oz) each
450–550 g (1–1¼ lb) fusilli
50 g (2 oz) butter

175 g (6 oz) shelled walnuts, broken into pieces
salt
freshly ground black pepper
45 ml (3 tablespoons) chopped fresh parsley

Cut Gorgonzola and mozzarella into small cubes, discarding rind. Cook fusilli for about 10 minutes in plenty of boiling, salted water. When they are almost cooked, melt the butter in a small pan, and add the walnuts. Coat well in butter, then leave to heat through thoroughly, whilst you drain the pasta.

Return well-drained pasta to the pan, and tip cheese on top, followed by walnuts and butter, parsley, and plenty of freshly ground pepper. Toss ingredients together and serve quickly.

## Salsa Normanno

**SUGGESTED MENU**

*Medaillons of
Avocado*

*Tomato Pasta with
Salsa Normanno*

*Green Salad*

*Raspberries with
Yogurt and
Demerara Sugar*

The garden of the Ristorante Normanno in Tropea in southern Italy looks out across the vine-clad ravine towards the dome of a half-ruined floodlit church. It is situated at the edge of the small 18th century Calabrian town. At the foot of the cliff, the clear Tyrrhenian sea laps at the shore. An idyllic spot. The food in the town is excellent, too. The Ristorante Normanno lays claim to a little more sophistication than other restaurants, but still uses pungent local ingredients to good effect. This brown-black olive-based sauce is one of the chef's specialities.

Dried tomatoes in oil are stocked by many Italian delicatessens – they may seem expensive, but invest when you can. The rich caramelised taste of concentrated sun-dried tomato is like nothing else. Serve a few with a selection of hams and salamis, and a bowl of black olives as a simple first course. Or dice and toss into hot fresh pasta with a couple of spoonfuls of oil from the jar, and a finely-chopped clove of garlic if desired. They can be used to zap up a simple cheese or ham sandwich, or served on baked *crostini* (see below) with drinks.

---

| | |
|---|---|
| 150 g (5 oz) black olives | 25 ml (1½ tablespoons) |
| 10 dried tomatoes | capers |
| 7 anchovy fillets | 90 ml (6 tablespoons) olive oil |

---

Slit the olives and remove stones. Liquidise with all remaining ingredients, to give a thick, slightly grainy paste. Serve on a bed of pasta (it looks very dramatic with orange tomato pasta), tossing it at the table, but keep back 2 or 3 tablespoonfuls and serve separately in a small bowl, for those who love the strong taste.

With any luck you may have some left over that could be used in either of the following ways:

**Cod Steaks Normanno** Smear cod steaks with *Salsa Normanno*, and grill until just cooked through. Serve with boiled new potatoes, and a green or tomato salad.

**Crostini Normanno** Oil a baking tray generously with olive oil. Spread one side of several thick slices of bread with *Salsa Normanno*, and place, paste side up on the tray. Bake in a hot oven until crisp. Serve with drinks, or as a simple first course.

Even simpler *crostini* (but still delicious) can be made by wiping the surfaces of the bread with the cut side of a halved clove of garlic. Place on a well oiled baking tray and dribble a little olive oil over uppermost surface. Bake as above. Serve on their own or with a few pieces of dried tomato.

## Cream, Mint and Lemon Sauce

The mint and the lemon give this plain cream sauce a breath of freshness. Serve it with tagliatelle, or taglierini, as a first course, or over filled tortellini, ravioli, or other pasta stuffed with spinach or chicken, or veal, as a main course. Forget about serving Parmesan with it – the flavours are far too delicate.

SUGGESTED MENU

*Poor Man's Asparagus*

*Tortellini with Cream, Mint and Lemon Sauce*

*Green Salad*

*Macédoine d'Ivoire*

| | |
|---|---|
| 40 g (1½ oz) butter | grated zest and juice of |
| a generous 300 ml (½ pint) | 1 lemon |
| of double cream | salt |
| 5 ml (1 teaspoon) dried mint, or | freshly ground black pepper |
| 15 ml (1 tablespoon) | |
| chopped fresh mint | |

Melt the butter in a frying pan. When bubbling, stir in cream, mint and lemon zest. Stir and leave to bubble for 5 minutes. Take off the heat, and when the bubbles subside, add lemon juice – start with half, and add more if necessary – salt and pepper.

Pour the sauce over hot cooked pasta, and serve immediately.

## Pasta with Mussels and Orange

SUGGESTED MENU

*Strawberry, Goat's
Cheese and White
Radish Salad*

*Pasta with Mussels
and Orange*

*Hot Chocolate and
Ginger Soufflé*

This is a wonderfully pretty dish – the orange of the mussels and the grated zest dotted about a mound of hot buttery white or green pasta. Cleaning the mussels takes time, though it is possible to get ones that have already had most of the barnacles and beard removed. They will still need picking over and rinsing with cold water. But once the mussels have been prepared, the final cooking takes only a few minutes.

| | |
|---|---|
| 1.4 kgs (3 lbs) mussels | 100 g (4 oz) butter |
| 2 oranges | 45 ml (3 tablespoons) |
| 700 g (1½ lbs) spaghetti or | chopped fresh parsley |
| tagliatelle | pepper |
| salt | |

First prepare the mussels. Wash and scrub them, removing any barnacles, and wispy bits of beard. Any open mussels that do not close when tapped should be thrown out. Put 60 ml (4 tablespoons) of water in a large pan, and add the mussels. Cover and place over a high flame. The mussels will start to open quickly in the steam – check after about 30 seconds. Remove the opened mussels from the pan. Discard any mussels that steadfastly refuse to open. Strain the liquid through a piece of muslin, and reserve. Take the mussels out of their shells, and set aside.

Finely grate the zest of the two oranges, taking care not to include any of the white pith – if you have a special zester, use that, to make thin curls. Heat up a large pan of salted water, and add the pasta. Meanwhile, melt the butter in a small pan, and add the juice of one of the oranges, the zest, and the strained cooking liquid from the mussels. Simmer together for 2 or 3 minutes.

When the pasta is nearly cooked, add mussels to the hot orange butter, and warm through quickly. Drain the pasta well as soon as it is *al dente*, and toss with mussels and juices, parsley, and lots of freshly ground pepper. Serve quickly.

## Other PASTA Recipes

**Spaghetti Carbonara con Porcini** *(page 115)*

**Two Mushroom Sauce** *(page 112)*

# EGGS

Lots of buttered soldiers, and the runny yolk of a soft-boiled egg to dip them into . . . mmm, what a pleasant thought. I now have a great urge to rush to the kitchen and put on a pan of boiling water. I've never understood why anybody should choose a hard-boiled egg for breakfast, when they could have had a soft-boiled one. If the small risk of salmonella poisoning is the culprit, then I would have thought it better to do without altogether.

The normally death-defyingly dull egg mayonnaise doesn't actually need to be so at all. With good homemade mayonnaise, flavoured with anchovy essence, or garlic, or lots of fresh herbs in the centre, and freshly-boiled eggs sliced and arranged thoughtfully around it, there is actually no reason at all why it shouldn't taste excellent and look very pretty. You might use a mixture of quails' and hens' eggs, or add a few strips of anchovy, some capers, or tomato.

I like eggs with smoked fish, too. One good combination is with smoked haddock in a spinach gratin. Prepare a double quantity of spinach as in the *Baked Eggs Florentine* recipe, and spread half in a thick layer in an ovenproof gratin dish. Next add a layer of flaked smoked haddock, topped with slices of hard-boiled egg. Spread the remaining spinach over the top, cover with breadcrumbs, dot with butter and bake in a moderate oven until browned.

On the same theme, eke out a small quantity of smoked salmon, by serving with a dozen hard-boiled quails' eggs, or a dish of cold scrambled eggs with chives, or lemon juice. Never add milk to scrambled eggs. Never overcook them, especially if you are to serve them cold – they continue to cook in their own heat for a while.

**Sublime scrambled eggs** For the best scrambled eggs, beat the eggs together well, and season. Melt a large knob of butter in a pan, and add the eggs. Stir over the lowest heat, until the eggs are thick and creamy, and then take straight off the heat, adjust the seasoning and transfer eggs to a cooler dish. Stir fresh herbs into the eggs as they cook. To get even better scrambled eggs, add a few tablespoons of cream as you beat the eggs. For lemony scrambled eggs, add the grated zest of a lemon, and a tablespoon or two of juice, plus some double cream, to the raw eggs. Cook slowly, adding more lemon juice if necessary.

And a final note on quails' eggs. I buy them in the supermarket, and they are relatively cheap and plentiful. They are small and enchantingly pretty, in or out of their shells. For the simplest of hors d'ouevre, serve lightly-boiled quails' eggs in their shells (cover with cold water, bring to the boil, and simmer for 30–60 seconds) with thin slices of brown bread and butter, and a bowl containing equal parts coarsely ground pepper, salt, and coarsely ground toasted cumin or coriander seeds, so the eggs can be shelled then dipped in the spices. Delicious.

# Baked Eggs

The perfect baked egg – white just set, smooth, creamy, and yolk lightly misted over, but runny and thick when the fork breaks through. Baked eggs have often been my solution to the problem of unexpected friends dropping in at around supper-time. Exactly what goes with them, around them, or under them, has depended on what is in the fridge or vegetable rack. In general allow one egg per person for a first course, two as a main course. Here is the basic method, followed by a few variations on the theme:

| | |
|---|---|
| 25 g (1 oz) butter plus extra for greasing dishes | 90 ml (6 tablespoons) whipping or double cream |
| 6 eggs | salt and freshly ground black pepper |

Grease either one large ovenproof dish, or 6 little ramekins. Heat the oven to 180°C (350°F) gas mark 4. Fill a roasting tin to a depth of 1cm (½ inch) with hot water. Set the dish(es) to heat through in the oven for 5 minutes.

Have all the ingredients standing by. Quickly whip the dish(es) out of the oven, and break the eggs in, one by one. Spoon cream over the top, then dot with butter. Bake for 10–12 minutes standing in the tray of hot water, until the white is just set. Season, and serve with triangles of fried or toasted bread.

**Baked Quails' Eggs** Many supermarkets now stock quails' eggs, so this isn't quite as chichi as it sounds. Allow 3 or 4 eggs per person, and cook as above, reducing cooking time to 6–8 minutes.

## Baked Eggs on Laverbread and Orange

Laver is a seaweed found around the shores of Wales amongst other places. Occasionally, a good fishmonger will sell it ready cooked and puréed, and then it is known as laver-bread. Laverbread is also available tinned. Serve this as a first course.

| | |
|---|---|
| 175 g (6 oz) laverbread | 6 eggs |
| juice of 1 orange | 25 g (1 oz) butter plus extra |
| salt and freshly ground black pepper | for greasing dishes |

Flavour laverbread with orange juice, salt and pepper. Grease one large dish or 6 small ramekins, and spread a thick layer of laverbread in each one.

Heat dish(es) through in the oven (see basic method), then break eggs in. Dot with butter and bake as for *Baked Eggs*.

## Baked Eggs on a Bed of Carrots and Leeks

| | |
|---|---|
| 225 g (½ lb) carrots, peeled | salt and freshly ground black pepper |
| 2 large leeks, washed | 25 g (1 oz) butter plus extra |
| 60–75 ml (4–5 tablespoons) double cream | for greasing dishes |
| pinch of dried thyme | 6 eggs |

Cut the carrots into julienne strips. Blanch in salted water until just tender. Remove outer layer of leeks, and cut into julienne strips. Again blanch in salted water until just tender. Drain carrots and leeks well, and mix with cream, thyme, salt and pepper.

Grease one large dish, or 6 small ramekins, and spread a thick layer of carrots and leeks on the bottom. Heat dish(es) through in the oven (see basic method), then break eggs in. Dot with butter, and bake as for *Baked Eggs*.

## Eggs Baked on a Bed of Black Salsify

It's not often that one comes across black salsify (scorzonera) or indeed ordinary salsify, but if you do see any for sale, snap it up quickly, particularly if it is a vegetable you are not familiar with. The long thin black roots are unmistakable, and the subtle flavour makes the slightly tedious process of peeling more than worthwhile.

| | |
|---|---|
| 450 g (1 lb) black salsify (or white if you can find it) | 5 ml (1 teaspoon) cornflour a sprig of fresh tarragon, or 5 ml (1 teaspoon) dried |
| 25 g (1 oz) butter plus extra for greasing dishes | salt and freshly ground black pepper |
| 150 g (5 oz) natural yogurt | 6 eggs |
| 75 ml (5 tablespoons) cream | |

First prepare the salsify: wash well, to remove as much as possible of the tenaciously clinging earth that inevitably accompanies these roots. If you have a pan large enough to hold the full length of the salsify, just top and tail. Otherwise halve – do not be alarmed by the sticky white juice that will ooze out. Drop them as quickly as possible into a pan of boiling salted water, and simmer until soft – this may take as little as 15 minutes if they are thin, up to 35 if they are thicker. Drain and run under the cold tap immediately, and peel as soon as possible.

Butter either one large ovenproof dish, or 6 ramekins. Cut salsify into 5-cm (2-inch) lengths, or smaller if necessary. Arrange in a single layer on the base of your dish(es). Beat the yogurt with cream, cornflour, tarragon, salt and pepper and pour over salsify. Heat in the oven for 5 minutes, break eggs carefully on top of salsify, dot with butter and bake as for *Baked Eggs*.

## Baked Eggs Florentine

---

700 g (1½ lb) fresh spinach, or 450 g (1 lb) frozen spinach
60–75ml (4–5 tablespoons) double cream
nutmeg

salt and freshly ground black pepper
25 g (1 oz) butter plus extra for greasing dishes
3 slices good cooked ham
6 eggs

---

Rinse fresh spinach well, discarding any damaged leaves. Pack into a large saucepan and stand over a low heat. Stir after 5 minutes, and raise heat for a moment if the spinach has exuded a lot of liquid. As soon as the spinach is cooked, drain well, then squeeze any remaining liquid out of the leaves. If you are using frozen spinach, cook as per packet instructions. Chop finely, and mix with cream, nutmeg, salt and pepper to taste.

Grease 6 ramekins, or a large ovenproof dish. Line with ham, then spread the spinach over the ham in a thick layer. Heat the dishes through in the oven (see basic method), break eggs in gently, dot with butter, and bake as for *Baked Eggs*.

# Poached Eggs on an Oatmeal Nest

The contrast of textures in this dish is very pleasing – soft crumbly oatmeal pastry, smooth white, runny egg yolk, and creamed spinach. If like me, you are not the world's greatest poacher of eggs, you could cheat, by coddling or boiling the egg for just long enough for the white to set properly, without the yolk thickening too much.

**6 eggs**

Pastry:
**75 g (3 oz) plain flour**
**75 g (3 oz) rolled oats**
**pinch of salt**
**75 g (3 oz) butter**
**1 egg, beaten**

Spinach Sauce:
**450 g (1 lb) fresh spinach, washed or 350 g (12 oz) frozen spinach**

**15 g (½ oz) butter**
**1 large clove of garlic, skinned and finely chopped**
**150 ml (¼ pint) double cream**
**lemon juice**
**salt and freshly ground black pepper**
**15 ml (1 tablespoon) finely chopped fresh parsley to serve**

Mix flour with oats and salt, then rub in the butter. Add enough beaten egg to form a soft pastry dough. Line 6 small tartlet tins with pastry and leave to relax in the fridge for half an hour. Prick with a fork, and line with greaseproof paper, weighted down with baking beans. Bake blind, at 190°C (375°F) gas mark 5 for 15 minutes until just beginning to colour.

Cook the spinach in the normal way (see *Baked Eggs Florentine*), and squeeze dry. Chop finely. Sauté garlic in butter, then add spinach and cream to the pan. Simmer together for three minutes, then season with lemon juice, salt and pepper.

Poach eggs. Put a spoonful of hot sauce in each tartlet, top with a poached egg, and pour a little more sauce over the top. Scatter with parsley, and serve quickly, passing remaining sauce round separately.

## Coconut Crème Brûlée

One of the great joys of a crème brûlée, is that moment when you shatter the smooth mirrored sugar surface, to expose the custard or cream underneath. The other great joy is, of course, eating it.

This is the traditional custard-based crème brûlée, made with coconut milk (available canned from Indian shops and some supermarkets), instead of cream and milk. Make the custard a day in advance, so that it has time to chill. A layer of fresh mango, underneath the coconut custard, is a delicious embellishment.

**SUGGESTED MENU**

*Smoked Chicken
and Pear Salad*

*Calves' Liver
Normande*

*Coconut Crème
Brûlée*

450 ml (14 fl oz) can of
    coconut milk
6 egg yolks

50 g (2 oz) caster sugar plus
    extra for top
pinch of salt

Warm the coconut milk. Beat the egg yolks with the sugar in a bowl, until light and fluffy. Add the salt and the warm coconut milk, and whisk in well. Place the bowl over a pan of simmering water, and stir until custard thickens enough to coat the back of a spoon.

Pour the custard into one large ovenproof dish, or 6 small ramekins. Stand in a roasting tin, and pour in enough water to come an inch or so up the side of the dish(es). Bake at 170°C (325°F) gas mark 3 for 12 minutes for a single large custard, 6 minutes for the small custards. Leave to cool, then chill.

Turn the grill to its highest setting, and let it get fiercely hot. Dredge the top of the custard(s) with an even layer of caster sugar, about 0.5 cm (¼ inch) thick. Stand them in the grill tray, or a roasting pan, and surround with ice (to keep the custard as cool as possible). Put them under the grill, as near as possible to the heat. Turn occasionally if the sugar is caramelising unevenly. When the sugar has caramelised, and turned brown, take the custards out, and leave to cool. Serve lightly chilled.

## Zabaglione Coffee

SUGGESTED MENU

*Tomato and Fennel Salad*

*Courgettes Paesana in Bread Cases*

*Zabaglione Coffee*

This was discovered by a friend of mine – a case of necessity being the mother of invention. Towards the end of a late meal in an Italian restaurant, the waiters admitted that they were quite out of milk, and cream. In desperation, Jess leaned across the table, scooped up a large spoonful of her companion's zabaglione, and poured it over her coffee. And yes, it was wonderful.

Traditionally zabaglione is made with Marsala, but all kinds of other alcohol can be used – brandy, Calvados, whisky (which will make it less sweet), or a good sweetish wine, such as a Moscatel, or Sauternes.

---

**4 egg yolks**
**50 g (2 oz) caster sugar**
**60ml (4 tablespoons) brandy,**
 **or Calvados or 120 ml**
 **(8 tablespoons) Marsala,**
 **Moscatel, or Sauternes**

**6 cups strong hot black**
 **coffee**

---

**P**ut the egg yolks, caster sugar, and alcohol into a large bowl. Whisk together then set bowl over a pan of simmering water. Keep whisking, until the mixture turns into a thick froth and triples in volume.

As soon as the coffee is ready, top each cup with a large swirl of zabaglione, and serve quickly.

## Other EGG Recipes

Cheese Mousse *(page 43)*

Timbales de Courgettes *(page 90)*

Tomato and Ricotta Soufflé *(page 128)*

Three Pepper Soufflé *(page 108)*

Medaillons of Avocado *(page 76)*

Spaghetti Carbonara con Porcini *(page 115)*

Gratin of Fresh Pears *(page 175)*

Elderflower Custard *(page 140)*

Hot Chocolate and Ginger Soufflé *(page 133)*

Red Fruit Gratin *(page 178)*

Vanilla Soufflé *(page 180)*

Apple and Pistachio Mousse *(page 149)*

# CHEESE

I was partly brought up in a small French village. For a child, it was an idyllic place. The village covered part of one of the slopes of the valley of the River Loir. A maze of narrow earth paths and stairways linked the only two tarred roads – one at the top of the hill, one at the foot. My friends and I had the run of an entire village, which was virtually carless. Like all good French children, I fetched the bread and croissants in the early morning, still warm from the baker's oven. And once or twice a week, I would cross the river, with my mother, to go to the dairy that made our local cheese – *Le Petit Trôo*.

Inside, the drip, drip, drip of draining whey, and row upon row of cheeses of varying age. We would pick a very young cheese, still soft and creamy, to eat with sugar or jam, and an adolescent with the first traces of a velvety white rind. Sometimes we would take, too, a more mature specimen – by now firm, with a pronounced flavour. One friend always kept his cheese until it was positively senile – wizened and shrunken, and as hard as a bullet. So, far from producing one simple cow's milk cheese, our little dairy offered a multiplicity of tastes and textures.

And at the top of the village was a farm selling fresh cream, milk and soft curd cheese, quite different from the *Petit Trôo*. My parents were never too convinced about the hygiene, or the friendliness of the farm dogs, but occasionally we would risk both for a bowl of the cool fresh curds to be mixed with garlic and herbs.

It's rare outside France, to be offered that kind of choice, but nonetheless, over the past few years there does seem to have been quite a cheese revolution. We'd had it drummed into us by large manufacturers that cheese arrives in neat plastic-wrapped cubes, but little by little real farmhouse cheeses have been infiltrating first the delicatessens, and now many supermarkets too. Gradually, it is becoming clear that real Cheddar, for instance, far from having a natural plasticky tang coupled with a sweaty texture, tastes nutty, and sharp and actually deserves its worldwide reputation.

**Good cheese** The coupling of science and traditional methods and knowledge, has given us a new and extraordinary range of *reliable* native cheeses. It's all very well to get misty-eyed and nostalgic about the cheeses of the past, and our lost heritage, but until this century, cleanliness and science did not always go hand in hand with country cheesemaking. There were marvellous cheeses, but output and quality were variable. As a result, only a few reached markets outside their area of origin, with any regularity.

More and more French cheeses are being imported now, so the choice in a good cheese shop can be quite bewildering. If you are pushed for time, it is obviously more sensible to round off a meal with cheese and fruit, than to try and conjure up three beautifully prepared and balanced courses. It is often rather nicer too. On the other hand, it is often rather more expensive. More and more, though, I think we've all realised that we don't have have to present a 'cheeseboard' with dozens of different cheeses, as if we were running a restaurant, rather than spending an enjoyable evening with friends over a good meal. Far better to search out one or two really first class cheeses, and present a couple of generous wedges, or whole rounds. Any uneaten remains should keep better, too – I hate finding tiny forgotten dog-eared packages of elderly cheese, lurking in gangs at the back of the fridge or larder. But one passably large piece of cheese could well be potted (see recipe for *Potted Stilton and Peppered Pears* (page 171) or turned into a *Cheese mousse* (see below). Or grated over fresh pasta – Parmesan is perfect and traditional, but that's no reason not to use other punchy cheeses – or turned into a soufflé, and frozen (see page108) ready for a later date.

## Crudités with Goat's Cheese Sauce

Many of the big supermarkets now stock smetana – it tastes like thick creamy buttermilk. If you can't buy it locally use *fromage blanc* or thick double cream instead.

SUGGESTED MENU

*Crudités with
Goat's Cheese Sauce*

*Fennel Siciliano*

*Strawberry and
Orange-Flower
Sorbet*

175g (6 oz) goat's cheese (I use Bûcheron)
200 ml (7 fl oz) smetana
15 ml (1 tablespoon) fresh mint or chervil, finely chopped
salt and freshly ground black pepper
12 quails' eggs
A selection of fresh vegetables, for instance:

2 large carrots
1 red pepper
1 green pepper
1 head of fennel
½ cucumber
3 sticks celery
Also good might be young green beans, lightly blanched if necessary, mange-touts, radishes, etc.

**M**ash the goat's cheese with the smetana. Use a blender if you like, though I prefer the rougher texture obtained with a fork. Stir in mint, salt and pepper to taste. Chill lightly before serving.

Put the eggs in a small pan, cover with water and bring to the boil. Simmer for 2 minutes and drain. Run under cold water, and peel when cool enough to handle. Prepare vegetables – peel carrots, seed peppers, remove the outer layer of fennel, string celery. Cut all vegetables into 7–10cm (3–4 inch) sticks. Arrange on a plate, with the eggs at the centre, and serve with the goat's cheese sauce.

# Brie Amandine

We all know how well apples and cheese go together – this recipe exploits that love-match. It is important that you serve a very plain water biscuit with the sizzling hot Brie to counteract the inevitable richness. I've always cooked this in an oval glazed earthenware dish, about 5 cm (2 inches) deep, and it's ideal.

**SUGGESTED MENU**

*Tomato and
Chickpea Soup
Brie Amandine
Orange Jellies*

---

550 g (1¼ lb) Brie
60 g (2 oz) slivered almonds
3 eating apples

40 g (1½ oz) butter
water biscuits to serve
    (e.g. Bath Olivers)

---

Cut the Brie into thin wedges (but do not cut off its rind), and pack into an ovenproof dish, leaving just a few gaps between wedges. Bake at 200°C (400°F) gas mark 6 for 25–30 minutes until cheese begins to brown.

Spread the almonds out on a baking tray and place in the oven, along with the cheese, to brown. Shake from time to time. Meanwhile, peel, core and quarter apples. Halve the slices, and fry in butter, until golden. As soon as everything is ready, arrange the apple slices round the edge of the Brie, scatter almonds over the top, and serve immediately, still bubbling, with the water biscuits to dip into the runny cheese.

## Grilled Goat's Cheese with Harlequin Salad

SUGGESTED MENU

*Grilled Goat's Cheese with Harlequin Salad*

*Fricassee of Chicken with Lemon and Basil*

*Macédoine d'Ivoire*

Even my local uninspired supermarket now sells slices of goat's cheese cut from a long log of Bûcheron. If you can get them, though, use small goat's cheeses such as the French rigottes. Adapt the salad to the season – the trio of radicchio, yellow pepper, and mange-touts looks so bright and pretty, and the combination of crispness, sweetness, and bitterness works particularly well with the cheese. Grilled goat's cheese can be served at either end of a meal, or indeed, as a quick, light lunch or supper dish.

6 thin slices of bread
6 small goat's cheeses
  (such as rigottes), or
  6 1 cm (½ inch) slices
  Bûcheron
12 very small (or 6 small –
  see recipe) sprigs of
  thyme or rosemary
olive oil for brushing
1 large head radicchio,
  washed

1 yellow pepper, thinly
  sliced
100 g (4 oz) crisp young
  mange-touts, topped and
  tailed
25 ml (1½ tablespoons)
  French dressing (see page
  102)
freshly ground black pepper

Toast one side only of bread. Halve whole cheeses and lay cut sides up on untoasted side of bread – if using slices of cheese, either way up will do – trimmed to extend only 0.5 cm (¼ inch) or so beyond cheese. Press a sprig of thyme or rosemary on to the surface of each cheese, and brush lightly with olive oil. Grill until cheese is melting, bubbly and lightly browned.

Meanwhile prepare salad. Coat radicchio leaves, pepper slices and mange-touts lightly in dressing, and arrange on 6 small plates, leaving room for cheese. Transfer cheese and bread to plates, twist the pepper mill quickly over each one, and serve immediately.

## Cheese Mousse

Orange Cheshire cheese gives this mousse a pretty pale coral colour, but in fact any good hard cheese (or a firm goat's cheese) could be used. If you use Gruyère or Emmenthal, try adding 10 ml (2 teaspoons) caraway seeds instead of nutmeg. Thyme is good with goat's cheese.

Serve either as a first course, on a bed of watercress, or frisée, or as an alternative to a cheese course or pudding. Counteract its richness with melba toast, plain water biscuits or oatcakes.

*Serves 8–10*

| | |
|---|---|
| 3 egg yolks | 15 g (½ oz) packet gelatine |
| 150 ml (¼ pint) single cream | 45 ml (3 tablespoons) hot |
| 100 g (4 oz) crumbled or | water |
| grated cheese | 4 egg whites |
| salt, freshly ground black | |
| pepper and nutmeg | |

Place the egg yolks and the cream in a small pan and stir over a very low heat until thick enough to coat the back of a spoon. Do not allow to boil. Remove from heat and add the cheese, stirring until melted. You may find you need to return the pan to the heat for a minute or so. Season generously. Dissolve the gelatine in the hot water, and stir into the cheese mixture. Leave to cool. As it begins to set, whip the egg whites until stiff and fold in. Taste and adjust seasonings. Pour into a greased 90 ml (1½ pint) mould or individual small moulds, and leave to set. Turn out carefully to serve.

SUGGESTED MENU

*Cheese Mousse*
*Calves' Liver*
*Normande*
*Simple Red Fruit*
*Gratin*

## Other CHEESE Recipes

Pasta with Cheese and Walnuts *(page 23)*

Fillets of Plaice Wrapped in Lettuce *(page 47)*

Chicken Breasts en Croûte *(page 65)*

Tomato and Ricotta Soufflé *(page 128)*

Three Pepper Soufflé *(page 108)*

Baked Pepper and Ricotta Parcels *(page 109)*

Avocado Gratin *(page 77)*

Fennel Risotto *(page 95)*

Spaghetti Carbonara con Porcini *(page 115)*

Aubergine Parmigiana with Porcini *(page 114)*

Fichi Ripieni *(page 154)*

Potted Stilton with Peppered Pears *(page 171)*

Raspberries and Cream Cheese on Almond Tartlets
*(page 177)*

Strawberry, Goat's Cheese and White Radish Salad
*(page 183)*

# FISH

The smell of fresh sardines, sizzling as they grill over an outdoor wood barbecue, is, for me, on a par with that of newly-roasted and ground coffee. Totally different, of course, but both the kind of smells that lure you irresistibly towards their source, taste buds keen and alert in anticipation.

Fresh mackerel, herrings, red mullet and all those small fish are also deliciously grillable. Get the fishmonger to scale and gut them, then all that's left to do is brush them with oil or melted butter, and leave them under a hot grill, turning when just cooked through to the bone. If they are very plump, make three or four diagonal slashes across the thickest parts, so that the heat reaches through. It's possible to buy special double-sided hinged fish-shaped wire grills, which make turning the fish much easier. For extra flavour, fill the stomach cavity with sprigs of herbs, and infuse a few more in the melting butter or oil, with which you are to brush the fish.

Any firm-fleshed fish can be cut into even-sized chunks and threaded on to a skewer with vegetables (partially pre-blanched if necessary), or scallops, or small squares of bacon. Cook under a medium-hot grill.

You might marinade them for an hour or so – try a mixture of lemon juice and olive oil, with crushed coriander seeds, and garlic, or the grated zest of an orange and its juice. For a hint of the East, mix rice wine, or very dry sherry, with sesame oil, light soy sauce, finely-chopped fresh ginger, garlic and spring onions.

Marinade, and grill whole fish steaks too – buy ones that are at most 2 cm (3/4 inch) thick, and grill on one side only.

Turning them might be disastrous, and they should be thin enough to cook through from the top. Whole steaks can be on the dry side. Brush them well with oil or butter, or marinade, or bake them, wrapped in silver foil.

Whole fish are good baked, wrapped in foil, or nestled on a bed of vegetables.

On top of the stove, fry fish steaks quickly in butter, and then deglaze the pan with wine, brandy, lemon juice, add double cream, and simmer for two or three minutes. Season.

**Making fish stock**  Fish stocks take a mere half an hour to make, and a well-reduced fish stock, heated through with double cream, and then seasoned, makes the best of all sauces for fish. To make the stock, ask your fishmonger for 1 kg (2 lbs) or so of fish trimmings, and bone. Put them in a large pan with a quartered onion, one or two sliced carrots, a sliced stick of celery and a leek. Add a bouquet garni, 2 glasses dry white wine, 15 ml (1 tablespoon) of white wine vinegar. Add enough water to cover, and bring gently to the boil. Simmer for 20 minutes, and strain well. That's it. Use the fish stock as is to make soup, or boil rapidly in a wide pan until reduced to about 150 ml (1/4 pint), and use for a sauce.

Smoked salmon is the obvious way to start a meal, when time is short, but money less so. I'm a sucker for smoked salmon, myself, but if you feel in need of greater originality, look out for the rather rarer, but equally good, smoked sturgeon. If you're celebrating and in the money, serve it with a small pile of real caviar – mother and baby, as it were – and soured cream with chives. Lumpfish caviar is a saner alternative, though the family connection is then lost.

Smoked eel, or trout are very nice too, and easier on the pocket. Serve with wedges of lemon, or a horseradish sauce. Mix equal quantities of prepared horseradish and whipped cream. Sharpen with a squeeze of lemon juice, and season. Eke out a small amount of smoked fish, by serving with scrambled egg, made with the addition of cream, and a squeeze of lemon juice. Serve it hot or cold.

## Fillets of Plaice Wrapped in Lettuce

Wrapped in dark green lettuce, pale ribs snaking round and spreading out like lace, these little fish parcels look quite enchanting. They are as pleasing to the palate as they are to the eye. The herb-scented cream cheese spills out as they are cut, so they need no sauce.

They can also be prepared in advance, and served cold. Slice thinly, and lay the green and white spirals on a bed of green salad stuffs, tossed in French dressing. Serve as a main or first course, in which case this will be enough for 10–12. Instead of plaice, fillets of whiting, or better by far, of sole might be used.

**SUGGESTED MENU**

*Warm Devilled Duck Salad*

*Fillets of Plaice Wrapped in Lettuce*

*Dried Fig and Orange Tart*

45 ml (3 tablespoons) finely chopped fresh herbs – parsley, chervil, chives, basil, tarragon
350 g (12 oz) cream cheese

salt
6 plaice fillets, weighing about 100 g (4 oz) each
1 round lettuce, washed

**B**eat herbs with cream cheese and salt and divide into 6 portions. Spread skinless side of each fillet evenly with a portion of the cream cheese. Roll up starting from head end.

Separate lettuce leaves, and blanch in boiling water for 30 seconds. Drain and run under the cold tap to refresh. Very carefully, spread a few leaves out flat on a board, or a work surface, and wrap a roll of plaice in lettuce, so that it is completely enclosed. Repeat with remaining leaves and rolls of plaice. Arrange in a single layer on a foil-lined steamer basket, and steam for 5–7 minutes, until a skewer slips easily through to the centre of the roll.

## Poisson Cru Niçois

SUGGESTED MENU

*Poisson Cru Niçois*
*Pepper and Ricotta Parcels*
*Fichi di Sardegna*

Really fresh fish is essential to this simple dish of marinaded strips of sea bass or salmon and scallops. Buy it from a reputable fishmonger, or from a specialist Japanese shop, where you should find an excellent choice of ready prepared fish.

If you are worried that guests may be iffy about eating raw fish, then just keep mum as you serve it – the marinade 'cooks' the fish, that is the flesh becomes opaque, so it is not immediately obvious that it is raw. The Japanese, after all, are doing very well on a diet that includes a lot of raw fish.

Adjust quantities to suit your pocket.

*Serves 6–10 as a first course, 4–6 as a main course.*

1 kg (2 lb) sea bass, filleted or 1 kg (2 lb) tail piece of salmon, filleted or a mixture of the two
6 scallops
4 lemons
150 ml (¼ pint) best olive oil, plus 90 ml (6 tablespoons)
10 ml (2 teaspoons) black peppercorns, lightly crushed
10 ml (2 teaspoons) coriander seeds, lightly crushed
12 sprigs fresh basil, or marjoram
1.25 ml (¼ teaspoon) salt
frisée, or mâche (lamb's lettuce) to serve

Cut the fish into long strips, or diamond shapes. Separate corals from whites of scallops, and halve whites if large. Spread fish and shellfish out in a large dish.

Cut thin strips of zest from three of the lemons. Place the juice of these lemons in a screw-top jar, with 150 ml (¼ pint) olive oil, the peppercorns, coriander seeds, half the basil, roughly chopped, and salt. Shake well to mix, then pour over the fish. Cover and leave in the fridge for 1–2 hours.

Drain fish, and arrange elegantly on one large or 6 individual plates, with frisée, lemon zest, remaining basil and a few of the peppercorns and coriander seeds from the marinade. Dribble remaining olive oil over the top. Cut the last lemon into 6 wedges and add to the ensemble. Serve with good bread.

## Fish Chowder with Pesto

SUGGESTED MENU

*Fish Chowder with
Pesto
Green Salad
Orange and
Campari Jellies*

Chowders are thick hearty main course soups, and this one is no exception. If you are looking for something sophisticated for an occasion when looks matter this is not it. Skip on to the next recipe.

It is, however, ideal if you are really short of time and the weather outside is cold and blustery. The recipe is open to plenty of variation, and should be seen as a guide rather than law. Instead of whiting, use any firm-fleshed fish – fresh tuna, swordfish, cod – or add shellfish. The most famous chowder of all is, after all, the American clam chowder, and mussels could be added as well. Open shellfish in a separate pan (see page 26) and add juices to chowder.

The vegetables, too, can be varied according to what is best on the market. The only essential ingredients are the onion, carrots, potatoes and bacon. The pesto, which will be available in most Italian delicatessens, gives it a lovely basil flavour and scent, but if for some sad reason, there is a shortage of pesto, add a bay leaf, and a generous pinch of thyme or oregano as the soup simmers.

1 large, or 2 medium, onions, skinned and sliced
50 g (2 oz) butter
8 rashers bacon, cut in strips
450 g (1 lb) carrots, scraped and sliced in 1 cm (½ inch) discs
5 sticks celery, cleaned and cut into 1 cm (½ inch) chunks
2 green peppers, seeded, and diced
450 g (1 lb) potatoes, peeled and cut in 1 cm (½ inch) cubes
50 g (2 oz) flour
1.1 litres (2 pints) milk
salt and freshly ground black pepper
350 g (12 oz) skinned whiting fillets
100g (4 oz) peeled cooked shrimps
25 ml (1½ tablespoons) pesto
freshly grated Parmesan or Cheddar to serve

Soften the onion in a large pan, in butter, without browning. Add the bacon, and stir until cooked. Tip in all the prepared vegetables, and stir to coat in butter. Sprinkle flour on top, and continue to stir for a good minute, so that flour is evenly distributed. Add milk, season lightly, and bring to the boil. Simmer for 10–15 minutes until vegetables are all just cooked, stirring occasionally, to make sure it doesn't catch on the bottom of the pan.

Meanwhile, cut the whiting into large cubes. Add to vegetables, with shrimps, and cook for a further 2 minutes. Remove from heat and stir in the pesto. Taste and adjust seasonings.

Serve with small bowls of extra pesto and Parmesan, and plenty of fresh crusty bread, or baked *crostini* (see page 25). Follow with a palate-cleansing green salad.

## Black-Burnt Fish Steaks

The black crust on these fish steaks is composed of a mixture of fiery spices, cooked on the hottest of cast iron griddles. If you don't own a cast-iron frying pan or griddle, they can be cooked under a well pre-heated grill or on an outdoor barbecue, though the result will be a patchier mixture of brown-red and black.

This recipe has been very much in vogue in America where they use in particular the native redfish. In fact, I have been told that it was so popular that the redfish population has been severely diminished. Luckily for the fish, it has now been superseded by other more fashionable recipes.

But it works well with any firm-fleshed fish – tuna, cod, swordfish, for instance – and I for one am not worried by being one step behind the Americans in the fashion stakes. Black-burnt fish tastes too good to be ignored.

**SUGGESTED MENU**

*Timbales de Courgettes with Salsa Cruda*

*Black-Burnt Fish Steaks*

*Macédoine d'Ivoire*

15 ml (1 tablespoon) paprika
10 ml (2 teaspoons) salt
5 ml (1 teaspoon) chilli
  powder
10 ml (2 teaspoons) black
  peppercorns
5 ml (1 teaspoon) dried
  thyme

5 ml (1 teaspoon) dried
  oregano
1/2 an onion, skinned, and
  coarsely chopped
2 cloves of garlic, skinned
  and chopped
6 fish steaks, about 2 cm
  (3/4 inch) thick
50 g (2 oz) butter

Grind or pound all the ingredients, except fish and butter, to a thick paste. Coat both sides of each steak thickly with the paste.

Heat a large cast-iron frying pan or griddle over a hot flame for at least 5 minutes. Melt the butter in a small pan, and keep warm. Place steaks in the frying pan, and turn over as soon as the underneath has blackened, which will be in a matter of seconds. When the other side is black, remove quickly from the pan, and turn off heat. Don't forget that the pan will remain hot enough to burn for some time. Pour the butter over the black-crusted fish, and serve with a cooling salad, such as the *Moroccan Orange and Mooli Salad* on page 166, or a tomato salad.

## Other FISH Recipes

**Cod Steaks Normanno** *(page 25)*

**Jansson's Temptation** *(page 120)*

**Smoked Salmon Gratin** *(page 121)*

**Medaillons of Avocado** *(page 76)*

**Avocado Gratin** *(page 77)*

# SHELLFISH AND CRUSTACEANS

If you live near a large fish-market, then you have the means of creating one of the most perfect meals imaginable, right there at your fingertips. A London-based friend confided that he has every intention of one day rising at crack of dawn on a Saturday morning and heading straight down to the busy Billingsgate fish-market. There he would buy quantities of oysters, and clams, sea urchins if there were any around, uncooked prawns, crab, lobster – the best of that morning's catch.

If you can cope with the early morning, then try it one day, otherwise, if you have a good fishmonger, you should be able to put together a similar dish – though some of the freshness may be lost, especially if you buy prawns, shrimps, and other crustaceans already cooked. Everyone (except those who can't cope with shellfish or crustaceans of any kind) enjoys tucking into a large dish of prawns, and it may be easier and more effective to concentrate on them alone. If you can get hold of raw ones, boil them for 5–7 minutes in a salty brine (add enough salt to the water for an egg to float in it). Shrimps need only a minute or two. Undercook and they will be soft, overcook and they become tough, so keep tasting as they cook.

**Moules marinières**   Once oysters were the food of the poor, ignored by the rich. Now that this situation has been reversed, the mussel has to some extent taken the oyster's place. On cold blustery days, a huge steaming bowl of moules marinières is a very happy event. It is one of the simplest fish

53

soups-cum-stews to prepare. Like all mussel dishes, the only trying part is the preparation of the mussels. But once that is done, the actual cooking takes minutes.

First tip the mussels into the sink, and turn on the cold tap. One by one, scrub the mussels under the running water, removing barnacles and bits of wispy beard with a small knife. Throw out any mussels that do not close when tapped (they are dead) or that have cracked shells (these may also be dead, or at least in a less than healthy condition). That's it. It sounds quick, but does take a fair amount of time.

For moules marinières, allow 450 g or a pound (both roughly the same as a pint) of mussels per person, less if it is to be served as a first course. For six people, pour half a bottle of dry white wine into a large pan. Add one onion finely chopped, two or three cloves of garlic, and plenty of parsley, and simmer together for five minutes. Tip the mussels in and clamp the lid on firmly. Shake the mussels occasionally and they should be ready and open within a few minutes. Chuck out any that refuse to open (they're dead as well). Keep the mussels warm and strain and season the juices. Pour over the mussels, and serve quickly. You might enrich the mussel juice with double cream, or thicken with egg yolks, or add a spoonful of caraway or fennel seeds with the onion, instead of the garlic, and again thicken with cream. Taste and add a spoonful of Pernod to reinforce the flavours. The sauce could also be flavoured with a touch of curry paste, but keep it subtle and don't overwhelm the flavour of the mussels.

Whatever you do, serve the mussels in a large tureen or bowl. Everyone picks the mussels out of their shells, discarding these into a second big bowl placed for that purpose in the centre of the table. Then drink the juices like soup, with lots of crusty bread for dunking and mopping up.

# Grilled Mussels

Use the ready-cleaned mussels that many fishmongers now sell. They do still need picking over at home, to remove the stray limpet, and whiskery beards, but they halve preparation time. You might feel that just half a dozen mussels each is too restrained, but the breadcrumbs add extra bulk, and the slice of bread underneath will have soaked up delicious buttery juices.

SUGGESTED MENU

*Grilled Mussels*
*Calves' Liver*
*Normande*
*Pear Ice Cream in*
*a Chocolate Robe*

1 kg (2 lb) mussels
50 g (2 oz) butter, softened
2 cloves of garlic, skinned
   and crushed
15 ml (1 tablespoon) finely
   chopped parsley

grated rind of half a lemon
30 ml (2 tablespoons) lemon
   juice
40 g (1½ oz) breadcrumbs
6 large slices of bread, about
   1½ cm (¾ inch) thick

Pick over the mussels, throwing out any that will not close when tapped. Throw out any cracked or really small mussels. You should be left with around 45 (or more). Heat the grill. Put half the mussels on a baking tray, and grill for 2–4 minutes until they open. Repeat with the second batch. Throw out any mussels that resolutely refuse to open under the heat. Leave to cool while you prepare the butter.

Mash butter with garlic, parsley, lemon rind and juice. With your fingers or a sharp-edged teaspoon, make 6 small evenly-spaced holes in each slice of bread. Lay on the trays used for mussels, so that they soak up any juices. Select the 36 biggest mussels. Discard one half of each shell. Smear a small knob of flavoured butter over each mussel, filling any cavities, and settle on to one of the holes. Cover each shell with breadcrumbs (don't worry if they spill over on to the bread). Dot with any remaining butter. Return to grill to brown. Serve immediately.

## Shellfish Risotto

**SUGGESTED MENU**

*Parma Ham with
Exotic Fruit
Shellfish Risotto
Zabaglione Coffee*

Base your purchases at the fishmonger's on the list below, but don't feel obliged to stick to it – you could substitute crab claws, razor clams, fresh shrimp, lobster, or any shellfish.

The quantities given are enough to make a substantial first course, or on the other hand a light main course. If you feel it is imperative to increase the bulk, I would suggest merely adding a little more rice and liquid unless you are feeling flush – shellfish doesn't come cheap these days. Don't be tempted to use any old rice. Italian Arborio rice absorbs plenty of liquid without losing its shape, to give a perfect risotto.

| | |
|---|---|
| 6 large raw prawns | 75 g (3 oz) butter |
| 6 scallops | 350 g (12 oz) Arborio rice |
| 450 g (1 lb) clams | 300 ml (1/2 pint) sweet |
| 450 g (1 lb) mussels | dessert wine, such as a |
| 6 shallots, or 3 small red | Moscatel |
| onions, skinned and | salt and freshly ground black |
| chopped | pepper |
| 2 cloves of garlic, skinned | fresh chopped parsley |
| and finely chopped | |

Soften the shallots and garlic in 50 g (2 oz) butter in a large pan. Add rice, and stir for 2 minutes. Pour in wine, and simmer gently until absorbed. Add 300 ml (1/2 pint) hot water, and continue to simmer until absorbed, stirring occasionally. Repeat until rice is just *al dente* – it should absorb around 900 ml (1 1/2 pints) liquid, and take between 20 and 30 minutes. Season.

Meanwhile, prepare shellfish. Open clams and mussels

over a high heat in a covered pan, with a few tablespoons of water. Throw out any that won't open. Add any juices exuded, to the liquid in the rice. Remove shells from all except a dozen or so mussels and clams, and remove the small black siphons from the clams. Halve scallop whites, and sauté, together with prawns, in remaining butter, until cooked. Chop scallop whites. Again, add any juices to the rice. Stir scallops, shelled mussels and clams into risotto. Scatter with parsley, and arrange prawns, remaining mussels and clams in their shells on top.

# Shellfish Stew

As with the shellfish risotto, the list of shellfish given below should not be seen as binding. Take the best that the fishmonger offers – use more mussels and fewer of the more expensive fish, if needs be. Or, to turn it into a main course dish, just increase the quantity of mussels.

*Serves 6–8 as a first course*

| | |
|---|---|
| **450 g (1 lb) mussels** | **2 leeks, cleaned and thinly** |
| **450 g (1 lb) small clams** | **sliced** |
| **2 shallots, or 1 small sweet** | **25 g (1 oz) butter** |
| **onion, skinned and finely** | **a pinch of saffron threads** |
| **chopped** | **6 scallops** |
| **2 large wine glasses white** | **175 g (6 oz) cooked peeled** |
| **wine** | **shrimps** |
| **bouquet garni** | **150 ml (¹/₄ pint) double** |
| **salt and freshly ground black** | **cream** |
| **pepper** | **15 ml (1 tablespoon) finely** |
| | **chopped parsley to serve** |

**SUGGESTED MENU**

*Apple and Celeriac Salad*

*Shellfish Stew (with extra mussels)*

*Rich Chocolate Ice Cream*

57

**F**irst clean the mussels. Discard any that will not close, or are damaged. Do the same with the clams. Place the shallots or onion in a large pan with the wine, the bouquet garni, salt and pepper. Simmer together for 5 minutes, then add the mussels. Cover and cook for 2 or 3 minutes until mussels open. Discard any that stay shut. Repeat with the clams. Strain the cooking liquid to remove any bits of grit. Take half the mussels and clams out of their shells.

Stew the leeks in the butter for 5 minutes, then add the strained juices. Simmer for 10 minutes. Add the saffron and simmer for a further 3 minutes.

Meanwhile, detach the corals from the whites of the scallops, and halve the whites if they are large. Add to the simmering liquid, and poach for 2 minutes. Finally, add all the other shellfish, and the double cream. Taste and adjust seasoning. Heat through well, and serve scattered with parsley. Make sure there is lots of good bread to mop up the juices.

### Other SHELLFISH Recipes

**Pasta with Mussels and Orange** *(page 26)*

**Poisson Cru Niçois** *(page 48)*

The stealthy intrusion of fresh free-range chickens among the ranks of their battery-reared cousins is reassuring. There is obviously a demand for them, and poulterers are responding. Hurray. Whether or not you are concerned about earlier lifestyles, there is no doubt that a bird that has had a chance to run around tastes a great deal better than its caged-up counterpart. In culinary terms, there can be little debate. Go for the free-range chicken every time – it's worth each extra penny.

Enough of moralising, and down to business. Throughout the recipes in this book, there is very little mention of chicken (or other) stock. This is for practical reasons only. A good stock will magically improve the flavour of sauces and soups, and should you have some to hand use it wherever appropriate.

But, the assumption that in every household there is always a regular supply of good home-made stock is just that, an assumption, and not a proven fact. I often find myself saving bones with the intention of making stock, and eventually – and regretfully – throwing them out. This is, by and large, due to lack of time rather than inclination. I know one doesn't have to stand over the stove throughout the duration, but one does have to be in the house, and keep an eye on the pan to prevent burning. It's a question of co-ordinating bones and time.

A good stock keeps well, reduced by boiling hard, and then freezing to give a home-made stock cube, but I tend to find that mine gets used up very quickly. Manufactured stock cubes are a possible alternative, but the dominant slightly chemical flavour is a poor and often disastrous alternative to the real thing. So I have only included recipes where stocks are not an absolute necessity.

A whole chicken doesn't take long to roast, and always looks interesting, despite being an everyday sort of meat. Its big advantage is that while it is contentedly cooking away in the oven, you can be preparing the rest of the meal, and a good sauce to go with it. Tarragon and chicken is one of those perfect and obvious combinations. Place a sprig of tarragon and an onion inside the chicken, and for the sauce just melt a knob of butter in a frying pan, whisk in some double cream, and some fresh or dried tarragon, and leave to bubble for five minutes. Stir in chicken juices, and season.

## Stuffings for chicken   I often use a risotto mixture

as a stuffing, but better still, the *Risotto di Porcini* on page 112. It can be prepared the evening before. Serve the stuffed chicken with the *Two Mushroom Sauce* (page 112). The *Fennel Risotto* (page 95) is good too. Surround the cooked chicken with slices of cooked fennel and a thick tomato sauce, or even the *Hot Fennel and Potato Salad* (page 97).

Chicken breasts, when you are very pushed for time, have one obvious advantage over a whole chicken – they take no time at all to cook. The disadvantage is that in many cases, they will need more last-minute attention in the kitchen. You can't have everything. There are a thousand and one ways to cook chicken breasts. Something as simple as marinading them for half an hour or so in olive oil, lemon, and garlic, and grilling or frying can be delicious. Or try a more orientalish marinade of sesame oil, fresh ginger, spring onion, and dry sherry. Use the marinade to baste while grilling.

# Smoked Chicken and Pear Salad

Smoked foods are big business these days and many delicatessens display a range of smoked poultry and game birds. Smoked chicken should be thought of, like smoked salmon, as a treat, for a simple lunch or supper with mayonnaise and a salad, or stretched, as in this recipe, with other ingredients to make a beautiful, and quick first course. Instead of chicken you might use slices of delicate pink smoked turkey, or splash out on tiny smoked quail. Olive oil can be used instead of nut oil.

**SUGGESTED MENU**

*Smoked Chicken and Pear Salad*

*Three Pepper Soufflé with a Tomato Salad, or Green Salad, and Steamed Buttered New Potatoes*

*Iced Mango and Cardamom Fool*

50 g (2 oz) hazelnuts
15 ml (1 tablespoon) white wine vinegar
30 ml (2 tablespoons) hazelnut oil
30 ml (2 tablespoons) grapeseed oil (or other tasteless oil)

2.5 ml (½ teaspoon) sugar
salt and freshly ground black pepper
4 ripe pears
1 smoked chicken
frisée lettuce

First toast the hazelnuts. Place them on a baking tray, and leave in a hot oven for 5–10 minutes until they begin to brown. Set aside until cool enough to handle.

Meanwhile, make vinaigrette by putting vinegar, oils, sugar, salt and pepper in a screw-top jar. Shake well together. Taste and adjust seasonings. Half a dozen or so at a time, rub the hazelnuts between the palms of the hands to remove the papery skins. Halve nuts.

Peel, core and slice pears thinly. Toss quickly in a little vinaigrette. Cut thighs and wings from the chicken, and slice the breast. Arrange alternate slices of chicken and pear on a bed of frisée on a large plate, with thighs and wings in centre. Scatter with toasted hazelnuts, and drizzle a little extra vinaigrette over everything. Save any remaining dressing for another salad – it will keep well in the fridge.

61

## Fricassee of Chicken with Lemon and Basil

**SUGGESTED MENU**

*Grilled Goat's
Cheese with
Harlequin Salad*

*Fricassee of
Chicken with
Lemon and Basil
served with Green
Taglierini*

*Macédoine d'Ivoire*

I always used to think of a fricassee as a way of using up leftover chicken – a dustbin recipe. And although you could adapt this for ready-cooked chicken (just add the chicken pieces with the the green peas towards the end), it is much nicer when you start from scratch. Far from being Monday's dustbin for the remains of Sunday lunch, it is a fresh and summery dish. Serve it with buttered spinach taglierini, or rice.

6 chicken breasts
15 ml (1½ tablespoons) olive oil
1 onion, skinned and finely chopped
75 g (3 oz) ground almonds
30 ml (2 tablespoons) finely chopped fresh basil, plus a few extra leaves to serve

salt
100 g (4 oz) frozen peas, defrosted
3 egg yolks
juice of 1½ lemons

Brown the chicken breasts in oil and remove from pan. Turn the heat down, add the onion and cook until soft without browning. Return the chicken to the pan with ground almonds, basil, and 1 pint of hot water. Simmer together gently for 10 minutes or until chicken is cooked through. Take the chicken from the pan, and arrange on a hot serving plate. Keep warm. Add salt and peas, and simmer for 1 more minute. Remove from heat.

Beat the egg yolks with lemon juice, and whisk in a tablespoon of the hot (but no longer boiling) sauce. Stir the egg mixture back into the sauce, and pour around chicken. Serve immediately, garnished with extra basil leaves.

# Chicken Livers with Almond and Garlic Sauce

The thick garlicky almond sauce derives from Spanish recipes. A little goes a long way . . . if you are feeling cautious, halve the quantity of garlic. Serve as a first course and follow with a robustly-flavoured main course. If you have any left over, don't throw it away – use a couple of spoonfuls to dress hot boiled or steamed potatoes next day.

**SUGGESTED MENU**

*Chicken Livers with Almond and Garlic Sauce*

*Aubergine Parmigiana with Porcini*

*Elderflower Sorbet*

| | |
|---|---|
| **65 g (2½ oz) ground almonds** | **juice of ½ lemon** |
| | **salt** |
| **40 g (1½ oz) wholemeal, or light rye breadcrumbs** | **paprika** |
| | **450 g (1 lb) chicken livers** |
| **1 large clove of garlic, skinned and roughly chopped** | **seasoned flour** |
| | **oil for frying** |
| **200 ml (7 fl oz) milk** | **frisée lettuce to serve** |

Place ground almonds, breadcrumbs and garlic in a liquidiser. Turn on, adding milk slowly until you obtain a thick sauce. Season with lemon juice, salt and paprika to taste. Set aside, and dust with a little more paprika to serve.

Pick over chicken livers and remove any greeny-yellow patches. Cut into quarters. Place a few frisée leaves on each of six small plates. Toss the chicken livers in seasoned flour, and shallow fry in hot oil for a few minutes or until lightly browned. Arrange on the frisée leaves and serve with the sauce in a separate bowl.

## Tandoori Chicken Kebabs

SUGGESTED MENU

*Crudités with
Pesto and Tofu
Sauce
Tandoori Chicken
Kebabs
Potted Stilton with
Peppered Pears*

This is a fairly mild aromatic version of the traditional Indian tandoori. It works well, not only for chicken, but also for firm-fleshed fish – try it with monkfish for instance. If you prefer a more fiery tandoori, increase the chilli powder to taste.

1 red pepper, seeded and cut into 2.5 cm (1 inch) squares
1 green pepper, seeded and cut into 2.5 cm (1 inch) squares
5 chicken breasts

Tandoori Marinade:
1 small onion, skinned and chopped
2.5 cm (1 inch) piece fresh ginger, peeled
1 clove of garlic, skinned
25 g (1 oz) butter
15 ml (1 tablespoon) coriander seeds
2.5 ml (½ teaspoon) black peppercorns

5 ml (1 teaspoon) green peppercorns
6 green cardamom pods
4 cloves
5 ml (1 teaspoon) turmeric
5 ml (1 teaspoon) salt
3.75 ml (¾ teaspoon) chilli powder
350 g (12 oz) natural yogurt

To Serve:
15 ml (1 tablespoon) chopped fresh coriander or mint leaves
225 g (8 oz) thick natural yogurt
1 lemon, cut into wedges

Cut the chicken breasts into 2.5 cm (1 inch) cubes. Liquidise all the marinade ingredients together, and coat the chicken well with the mixture. Cover and leave in a cool place to absorb flavours, for 1–2 hours.

Mix the coriander leaves in the yogurt. Thread alternate pieces of chicken and red and green pepper on to 12 skewers. Grill under a hot grill, turning as each side browns, until chicken is just cooked.

Serve kebabs, surrounded by lemon wedges, and with a bowl of yogurt and coriander.

# Chicken Breasts en Croûte

Home-made puff pastry would obviously be best for this recipe, but let's face it, it's a time-consuming job best saved for a leisurely weekend. Ready-made is (on the whole) a passable second best, and particularly useful are the thin sheets of frozen puff pastry that thaw individually in a matter of minutes – use six for the following recipe. If you can't lay your hands on fresh mint or parsley, substitute other fresh herbs rather than dried (e.g. chives, coriander, marjoram or chervil).

SUGGESTED MENU

*Iced Lemon
Fennel Soup*

*Chicken Breasts en
Croûte*

*Gratin of Fresh
Pears*

225 g (8 oz) cottage cheese
15 ml (1 tablespoon)
  chopped fresh mint
15 ml (1 tablespoon)
  chopped fresh basil
15 ml (1 tablespoon)
  chopped fresh parsley

salt and freshly ground black
  pepper
6 chicken breasts
450 g (1 lb) puff pastry
1 egg, beaten
75 g (3 oz) butter

Sieve the cottage cheese. Mix the herbs, and beat two-thirds of them into the cottage cheese, with salt and pepper. Make a deep slit in the side of each chicken breast, and fill with cottage cheese and herbs.

Lightly grease a baking tray. Divide the pastry into six. Roll out each portion into a rectangle. Lay a stuffed breast in the centre of the first rectangle and wrap in pastry, brushing edges with beaten egg, and pressing to seal. Repeat with each portion. Use any remaining pastry to make leaves, flowers or whatever to decorate. Place pastry parcels on the baking tray, seams underneath, and brush with egg. Bake at 230°C (450°F) gas mark 8 for 15 minutes, until pastry is beginning to brown. Lower the heat to 190°C (375°F) gas mark 5, and cook for a further 15 minutes. Test with a skewer to see if the breasts are cooked – the juices that run out should be colourless.

Meanwhile, melt the butter and add the remaining herbs. Leave over a very low heat until the chicken is ready. Serve each puff pastry parcel alongside a small pool of herby butter.

## Sweetcorn Pancakes with Chicken Livers and Sour Cream

SUGGESTED MENU

*Sweetcorn Pancakes with Chicken Livers and Sour Cream*

*Spinach Gratin with Smoked Haddock and Eggs*

*Slices of Orange Marinated in Cointreau*

This combination of hot sweetcorn fritters and chicken livers, and cold soured cream is particularly good, and wonderfully simple. If you wanted to make it simpler still, you could forget the chicken livers completely, and instead top each pancake with black or red lumpfish caviar – one small jar would be ample.

| | |
|---|---|
| 100 g (4 oz) cooked sweetcorn or frozen sweetcorn, defrosted | 15 ml (1 tablespoon) finely chopped fresh chives |
| 2 eggs | 150 ml (¼ pint) soured cream |
| 50 g (2 oz) flour | 100 g (4 oz) chicken livers |
| salt and freshly ground black pepper | 40 g (1½ oz) butter |
| | 15 ml (1 tablespoon) finely chopped fresh parsley |

Liquidise sweetcorn with eggs. Stir in flour, salt and pepper. Fold chives into the soured cream and chill. Pick over chicken livers, removing any greeny-yellow bits and cut into quarters.

Melt half of the butter in a frying pan, and when foaming drop in several tablespoons of sweetcorn batter, well spaced out. Fry until underneath is lightly browned, then turn and fry for a further minute. Drain on kitchen paper, and keep warm. Repeat until all batter is used. This should make at least 12 small fritters.

Add remaining butter to pan, and fry chicken livers quickly. Stir in parsley, and season. Place 2 hot pancakes on each plate, top with a dollop of chilled sour cream, and divide the chicken livers between the plates.

### Other CHICKEN Recipes

**Roast Poussins with Red and Green Sauces** *(page 129)*
**Avocado and Peach Chicken Kebabs** *(page 75)*
**Almond Roulade with Chicken and Mango** *(page 159)*

# DUCK

I have a small collection of ducks that sit on a windowsill. Not live ones, nor at all edible. One is a Korean marriage duck, two more are also oriental, carved from sandstone, but the fourth has a very solid European gait. He's old and wooden, but too small, I think, to have been made as a decoy duck for hunting.

I've always loved those life-sized decoy ducks – some rough and awkwardly carved, others intricate and detailed down to the last feather. In France, you can now buy plastic decoys, stuck on the end of a long stick, which is pushed down amongst the reeds and mud of the river, to lure unsuspecting ducks to a sorry end.

When you do see wild duck for sale, though, buy it in preference to farmed. The flavour is gamey without being fearsome, and it is much less fatty, having led a more energetic life. Check that it is not too old – the webbing of the feet should be soft, the breast plump.

The mallard is the one you are most likely to come across, and you will probably need two at a pinch, or three to feed six people well. Place a knob of butter mashed with herbs, or an onion, or an orange and/or lightly crushed juniper berries, in the central cavity. Allow about 15 minutes to 450 g (1 lb) (or even less if you like your duck very pink), in a very hot oven, 230°C (450°F) gas mark 8, and baste frequently with melted butter. If you've included juniper berries, you might baste with a mixture of gin and butter, to emphasise the flavour.

Although the roast duck recipes below are written for domesticated birds, they can easily be adapted to wild ducks, by reducing the cooking times. The sweetness of the sauces goes well with the stronger meat, as well as with the more muted and fatty flesh of the domesticated duck.

One large domesticated duck will just feed six, though with nothing but the bare bones left over. You may feel that two smaller 1.8 kg (4 lb) ducklings might be more generous. Again, allow about 15 minutes to 450 g (1 lb), in a medium hot oven.

*Magret de canard*, or sometimes even *Maigret* like the detective, has become increasingly popular on restaurant menus. Strictly speaking, it should be the breast of a duck that had been fattened for foie gras, but the breast of an ordinary common or garden duck often stands in. The simplest way to cook duck breasts is to skin and grill them medium rare, brushing first with oil. Serve neat as they are, with a little greenery and a few cherry tomatoes, or with the *Green Pea Sauce* on page 130.

The breasts can also be quickly fried, with skin, in a little butter, and kept warm whilst the pan is deglazed with port, or brandy, and then simmered with cream for a few minutes. If you slice the breasts thinly, and arrange them elegantly on a pool of sauce, with a few watercress leaves, then two will feed 4 as a first course.

# Duck with Sweet and Sour Onions

This is one of my favourite ways of cooking duck, surrounded by melting sweet and sour onions, that provide both sauce and vegetable. The onions are cooked quite independently of the duck, so there's no reason why they shouldn't be served without it, in their own right, or with other meats.

SUGGESTED MENU

*Medaillons of Avocado*
*Duck with Sweet and Sour Onions*
*Fresh Fruit*

2.5 kg (6 lb) duckling
salt
1 onion, skinned

Sauce:
450 g (1 lb) onions, skinned and thinly sliced
50 g (2 oz) butter
grated rind and juice of 1 lemon
50 g (2 oz) sugar

15 ml (1 tablespoon) clear honey
15 ml (1 tablespoon) raspberry or cider vinegar
pinch of ground nutmeg
pinch of ground ginger
pinch of ground cinnamon
salt and freshly ground black pepper

Wipe the skin of the duck, and prick with a sharp fork. Rub with salt and place the onion in the stomach cavity. Roast upside-down on a wire rack over a roasting pan at 190°C (370°F) gas mark 5 for 45 minutes. Turn right way up and roast for a further 45 minutes until cooked.

Meanwhile, make the sauce. Soften the onions slowly in the butter in a large pan, without browning. Add the remaining ingredients and enough water to just cover. Simmer, covered, for 20 minutes. Remove lid and simmer for a further 10 to 20 minutes until only a third of the original volume of liquid remains. Set aside until duck is cooked.

Serve duck surrounded by the onions, reheated if necessary.

# Duck with Marmalade Sauce

One might call this the 'cheat's Duck à l'Orange', if it weren't for the fact that it is actually rather nicer than nine out of ten versions of that over-exposed restaurant fall-back.

Use one of the high fruit content 'extra' jams or better still a completely sugar-free marmalade from a healthfood shop.

---

| | |
|---|---|
| 2.5 kg (6 lb) duck | 150 ml (¼ pint) double |
| 1 orange | cream |
| 175 g (6 oz) fine cut | 7.5 ml (1½ teaspoons) |
| marmalade | sugar |
| 150 ml (¼ pint) orange juice | salt and freshly ground |
| 150 ml (¼ pint) chicken | black pepper |
| stock or water and ¼ | |
| chicken stock cube | |

---

Wipe the duck and prick all over with a sharp-pronged fork. Halve the orange, and place both halves in the central cavity. Smear the duck with one tablespoon of marmalade (use your hands – it's sticky but much easier). Roast on a wire rack or trivet over a roasting pan for up to 1½ hours at 190°C (375 °F) gas mark 5, until cooked. Check from time to time, and if the marmalade is blackening too fast, cover with foil. Aim to finish up with a very dark brown duck, with the odd piece of orange, caught and slightly blackened by the heat.

To make the sauce, put the remaining marmalade, orange juice, stock and sugar into a saucepan and gently bring to the boil. Simmer together for 10 minutes, checking occasionally to make sure it isn't burning on the bottom of the pan. (If you are using a sugar-free jam this is much less likely to happen.)

When the duck is cooked, reheat the sauce if necessary, remove from heat and allow to cool for a minute or so. Then stir in cream and season.

## Devilled Duck Salad

Theoretically, this is a recipe for left-over cooked duck meat, but that is something I very rarely seem to have. A duck, after all, is not a turkey – it is not built to feed the multitude, and it tastes a lot better. I count myself lucky to have the bare carcass left over, picked quite clean, to make stock. So I would suggest that you buy a small duck, and cook it the night before.

The salad that accompanies the duck should be bright and colourful – below I suggest some wintery salad ingredients, but be guided by whatever looks best in the shops. The only items that are essential, in my opinion, are the cucumber and the tomatoes – their coolness balances the spiciness of the devilling, and the bright red dots of tomato liven up the potentially drab brown duck meat.

**225–350 g (8–12 oz) cooked duck meat**

Marinade:
**15 ml (1 tablespoon) mango chutney**
**15 ml (1 tablespoon) Dijon mustard**
**10 ml (2 teaspoons) Worcestershire sauce**
**15 ml (1 tablespoon) syrup from a jar of stem ginger**
**15 ml (1 tablespoon) olive oil**

Salad:
**2 tomatoes**
**3 heads chicory**
**2 large carrots**
**2 green peppers**
**½ cucumber**
**pinch of sugar**
**salt**

Tear the duck meat into roughly equal-sized small pieces. Beat the marinade ingredients together. Pour over the duck, turning meat so that it is well coated. Set aside for half an hour.

Prepare the salad – pour boiling water over the tomatoes, leave for 30 seconds and drain. Skin and seed tomatoes. Dice finely, sprinkle with a pinch of sugar, and a little salt, and chill. Peel the carrots, and cut into julienne strips. Cut peppers and cucumber into strips. Cut off bases of chicory heads, and separate the leaves, discarding any that are unusable. Arrange all except tomatoes on a large plate, or 6 small plates, leaving space to add the duck meat.

Line a grill pan with foil, and lay duck pieces on it in a single layer. Place under a very hot grill until beginning to brown, then turn pieces over with tongs, and brown the other side. If circumstances have landed you with lots of very small fiddly pieces, it may be difficult to turn them all over – don't worry, the meat is already cooked so just make sure it is hot and sizzling. Add the meat to the salad, and scatter with the diced tomato. Serve quickly.

# AVOCADOS

I don't know about you, but it seems to me that avocados are getting smaller and smaller, as they become easier and easier to buy. It's as if there were a limited quota of avocado flesh, so in order to meet the increasing demand, each avocado has to be suitably reduced in size. A silly supposition I know, since many of the smaller varieties of avocados have a better flavour than the larger ones, but I do get so annoyed by having to search for the two spoonfuls of flesh that surround the stone. On the other hand, and this isn't the contradiction it may at first seem, I'm all for the tiny elongated 'cocktail' avocados that one occasionally comes across. The difference is that these don't have any stones at all, so once you've penetrated the skin it's all yours. You serve several per person.

Their other big advantage is that, since they are stoneless, there is absolutely no temptation whatsoever to try and grow cute little avocado trees from the stones. Now, if you have half a dozen green leafy specimens sitting smugly on your windowsill, then you will probably disagree with me on this point. But, I have never had any success. I've tried every method going, and the best I've ever managed is one solitary sprout that died as soon as any leaves threatened to appear. I now feel guilty when I throw out an avocado stone – I shouldn't let them beat me – and an utter failure yet again, when I face up to the fact that what I thought might be roots, is actually rampant mould. Ho, hum. It's a good thing I didn't take up horticulture as a career.

**Ripening avocados** If you intend to serve avocados, buy them a couple of days in advance. A ripe avocado should give slightly when squeezed, and can be kept for three or four days in the salad compartment of the fridge. Often though, you may find that the only available avocados are hard and unripe, and quite unready to be eaten. If time is short, put them in a brown paper bag with an apple, banana or potato, and you will find that they ripen quickly. Otherwise, leave them in a warm room, and within a few days they will be ready to eat.

Turn the cut sides of avocado in lemon juice to prevent discoloration, but even so, don't prepare too long in advance, as the preventative effect of the lemon juice has only a limited lifetime. The simplest way of serving avocados is halved with a vinaigrette, but I think it prettier to peel them first, then cut into thin slices, tossed in vinaigrette, and arrange on a large plate. Scatter with fresh herbs. Expand on this theme by adding slices of mozarella and tomato, olives, and maybe a few thin curls of Parma ham. Smoked chicken or turkey mixes well with avocado in a salad, or try alternate slices of avocado and papaya. Whatever you mix with it, remember to add the essential sharp note of a French dressing, and pepper.

Chilled avocado soup takes seconds to make – liquidise avocado flesh with yogurt, and enough water, or better still, chicken stock, to give a thick cream. Season with salt, cayenne and a pinch of sugar, sharpen with lemon juice if necessary, and add lots of fresh chives or basil. A similar avocado sauce can be made by omitting the water and adding a hint of garlic or chopped sweet onion. Serve it cold with crudités, and cold or warmed (without boiling), with fish or chicken. Or use mashed seasoned avocado to stuff a chicken breast (see the recipe for *Chicken Breasts en Croûte*, page 65).

# Avocado and Peach Chicken Kebabs

Avocado and chicken, peach and chicken, avocado and peach – they all go together well. Here they are alternated on kebabs – bright flashes of green and orange against the pale chicken. Be sure to use only ripe fruits for these kebabs.

---

4 chicken breasts, skinned
juice of 1 lemon
juice of 1 orange
90 ml (6 tablespoons) olive
   oil
5 or 6 sprigs of fresh
   coriander or parsley,
   roughly chopped

10 ml (2 teaspoons) crushed
   coriander seeds
freshly ground black pepper
2 ripe avocados
2 ripe peaches
salt

---

Cut the chicken breasts into 2.5 cm (1 inch) cubes. Mix the lemon and orange juices with the olive oil, herbs, coriander seeds and pepper, and pour over chicken. Leave in a cool place for 1–2 hours.

Peel the avocados and cube. Add them quickly to the marinade, and coat to prevent discoloration. Pour boiling water over the peaches, leave for 30 seconds and drain, then skin and cube.

Thread half the chicken cubes on to 6 skewers, alternating with pieces of avocado. Thread the remaining chicken on to another 6 skewers alternating with pieces of peach. Grill under a medium grill for about 10 minutes, basting with the marinade, and turning occasionally, until lightly browned and cooked through. Season with salt, serve on a bed of buttered rice flecked with lots of herbs.

## Medaillons of Avocado

Medaillons, little medals – it sounds prettier than canapés, and these little circles of avocado, topped with smoked salmon, quails' eggs, and caviar, even if it is only lumpfish caviar, do look very pretty. If you can't get the quails' eggs, then either increase quantities of salmon and caviar, or substitute twists of Parma ham.

Pass them round before people actually sit down to eat – canapés/medaillons don't need plates – fingers and paper napkins should be quite enough and they cut down on the washing up.

9–12 thin slices of brown
  bread
25 g (1 oz) softened butter
100 g (4 oz) smoked salmon
1 lemon
90 ml (6 tablespoons) soured
  cream
salt and freshly ground black
  pepper

15 ml (1 tablespoon) finely
  chopped chives
2 large or 3 small
  avocados
12 quails' eggs
butter for frying
60 ml (4 tablespoons)
  lumpfish (or real)
  caviar

Toast bread lightly on both sides, and cut out 36 small circles, roughly 5 cm (2 inches) diameter. Cover and set aside. When cool, butter thinly. Cut a dozen circles, the same size, of smoked salmon. Cut the zest off the lemon in long strips. Season soured cream with salt and pepper and add the chives.

Peel the avocados, and slice thinly, turning in lemon juice. Cut into pieces that will just sit nicely on top of the bread circles. Fry the quails' eggs in the butter.

Quickly assemble the medaillons – top the bread circles with a piece of avocado. On top of 12 of them, place a dollop

of soured cream, topped with a little caviar. On the next 12, lay
a piece of smoked salmon, season with pepper and a squeeze
of lemon juice, and decorate with a curl of lemon zest. Finally,
lay quails' eggs on remaining circles, and season with salt and
pepper.

Arrange on a large plate, and pass round.

## Avocado Gratin

This is a marvellously quick and basic gratin, and yet
very, very good. It can be served as a first course, or
the quantities suitably increased, as a main course. It
can be made without the smoked fish, if you are cooking
for fish-free vegetarians.

SUGGESTED MENU

*Avocado Gratin*
*Roast Partridge
with Mexican
Chocolate Sauce*
*Raspberries with
Bay Cream*

2 smoked mackerel fillets, or
  smoked eel
3 ripe avocados
juice of 1 lemon
salt and freshly ground
  pepper

60 ml (4 tablespoons) olive
  oil
25 g (1 oz) Parmesan, freshly
  grated

With a fork, pull the mackerel into large flakes. Halve and
peel the avocados. Slice thinly, and turn the slices in
lemon juice. Arrange avocados and mackerel in an ovenproof
dish (or 6 individual, ovenproof ramekins), and pour over olive
oil. Season, then scatter Parmesan generously over the top.
Bake at 220°C (425°F) gas mark 7 for 25–30 minutes until
lightly browned. Alternatively, if the avocado and mackerel are
arranged in a thin layer, brown under a hot grill.

## Avocado and Orange Salad

**SUGGESTED MENU**

*Avocado and
Orange Salad*

*Salsa Normanno
on Spaghetti*

*Yogurt and
Demerara-Topped
Raspberries*

The dressing for this simple avocado and orange salad is
best made with a combination of ordinary orange and
bitter Seville orange juice, but that would limit it to the
few short winter weeks when Seville oranges are available.
At other times, I suggest you substitute the juice of half a
lemon instead, and add a little more sweet orange juice.

Serve as a first course – rather more interesting than just
plain old avocado vinaigrette.

---

1 Seville orange, or
  ½ lemon
3 sweet oranges
5 ml (1 teaspoon) black
  peppercorns, lightly
  crushed
5 ml (1 teaspoon) coriander
  seeds, lightly crushed
40 g (1½ oz) caster sugar

30 ml (2 tablespoons) olive
  oil
salt
3 large avocados
bunch of watercress or finely
  chopped fresh parsley
50 g (2 oz) pitted black
  olives, halved

---

Squeeze the juice of the Seville orange or lemon and
one of the sweet oranges. Place in a pan with the
peppercorns, the coriander seeds, and the sugar. Bring gently
to the boil and simmer for 5 minutes. Off the heat, beat in the
olive oil and salt to taste. Leave to cool.

Peel the avocados. Halve and remove stone, and cut into
thin slices, and turn immediately in the orange dressing. Slice
the remaining sweet oranges very thinly, zest, pith and all.
Arrange the avocado and orange slices with the watercress in
concentric circles on a large plate, and sprinkle with a little
more dressing, and some of the peppercorns and coriander
seeds. If not using watercress, scatter with parsley and olives,
and serve at room temperature, or lightly chilled.

## Avocado Fool

The first time I ate an avocado fool was in a Malaysian restaurant in London's Soho. The person sitting next to me was digging into an extraordinary mountainous confection of fluorescent pink and green. At its heart was a most peculiar selection of things – beans, lychees and more pink jelly. He assured me that it tasted much less frightening than it looked, but I felt that I had got the best of the deal, with my relatively simple avocado fool.

It is though, a rather unusual pudding – but rest assured, everyone I've tried it out on has liked it. The quantities given are certainly enough to feed eight as it is very rich. However, if you wish to serve it in the avocado shells, you will, of course, only have six containers . . . Whatever way you decide to present it (it also looks very pretty in plain, small ramekins) do eat it within a few hours of whizzing it up. The lemon juice prevents discoloration for a while, but after about 5 or 6 hours, it will begin to look slightly murky.

*Serves 8*

**SUGGESTED MENU**

*Baked Eggs
Florentine*

*Black-Burnt Fish
Steaks*

*Avocado Fool*

3 avocados
275 g (10 oz) fromage blanc
75 ml (5 tablespoons) clear
   honey
25–30 ml (1½–2 tablespoons)
   lemon juice

2 sesame crunch bars or 2
   tablespoons toasted
   flaked almonds
lemon zest to serve

Halve the avocados and scoop out the flesh, being careful not to pierce the skins if you are to serve fool in them. Quickly liquidise (or mash with a fork) avocado flesh with

79

*fromage blanc*, honey, and lemon juice. Taste and add more honey and lemon juice if necessary (it shouldn't be too sweet). Divide amongst the skins, or small bowls.

Crush the sesame crunch bars if using with a rolling pin, or pestle and mortar, and scatter the sesame crumbs or almonds over the fool, along with a few long strands or curls of lemon zest. Chill lightly before serving.

# CAULIFLOWER

In years gone by, I have been heard to slander cauliflower. To grimace, screwing up my face, no doubt grotesquely, and say 'ugh' at the very mention of the vegetable. For years I was quite convinced that I loathed it beyond measure. The culprit and cause of this loathing was, once again, odious school dinners, in particular the dreaded cauliflower cheese in its gluey sauce.

But now, I can enjoy the creamy white florets. Worries must still linger in my sub-conscious – I will rarely boil cauliflower, preferring to eat it raw, or steamed, thus minimising the chances of overcooking, whereby you lose a considerable percentage of the vitamins, and ruin the look, not to mention the taste.

That's such a shame, as it is such a decorative vegetable, with its ivory centre, and green leaves, one of the prettiest members of the cabbage family, which includes Brussels sprouts, kale, kohlrabi, radishes and turnips. Broccoli is in there too, and perhaps closest of all to the cauliflower – it's un-identical twin maybe? In Italy, I have come across what looks like a cross between the two: stunning near-fluorescent green-centred cauliflower, compact in the same manner as the ordinary variety, but with conical hills jutting out an inch or less from the surface. Piled up high on a stall in a narrow Roman street in December, they provided a thrilling burst of colour.

## Variations on cauliflower cheese If you are not traumatised by childhood memories, then try making a

Parmesan-flavoured and olive oil-based white sauce to go with cauliflower. Brown it under the grill, or bake in a hot oven, topped by a layer of breadcrumbs and a dribble of olive oil for half an hour or so. Simpler still, cook cauliflower florets, until barely *al dente*, layer in an ovenproof dish and dot with butter and Parmesan. Again, finish with breadcrumbs, and melted butter and bake. Alternatively make a quick buttery anchovy sauce by frying half a dozen anchovy fillets in lots of butter until they begin to dissolve. Mash anchovies into the butter, then toss cauliflower in a few spoonfuls and serve, or turn again to the breadcrumbs. A final mention of breadcrumbs, sauté a handful in butter or olive oil until golden brown, and scatter, with finely-chopped parsley, over cooked cauliflower – an old and well-known idea, but easily overlooked for all that.

Raw cauliflower salads are more than welcome in winter – toss simply in a French dressing, adding a handful of fresh herbs. Or use a flavoured vinegar, or nut oil – maybe add a few whole nuts as well. I like cauliflower with apple, or a few defrosted frozen peas (better still young unfrozen peas, but those can be difficult to get and take time to pod). Anchovy and anchovy-flavoured mayonnaise or vinaigrette goes well, too. Like leeks, you might also toss hot cooked cauliflower in dressing and serve cold, with chopped hard-boiled egg and chives.

# Stir-Fried Cauliflower

1 head of cauliflower broken into small florets
45 ml (3 tablespoons) sesame seed oil
2.5 cm (1 inch) piece of root ginger, peeled and finely chopped
1 large clove garlic, skinned and finely chopped
15 ml (1 tablespoon) sesame seeds
75 ml (3 fl oz) sherry
5 ml (1 teaspoon) soy sauce
10 ml (2 teaspoons) soft brown sugar
2 spring onions, chopped

**SUGGESTED MENU**

*Elona Salad with Parma Ham*

*Tomato and Ricotta Soufflé with Stir-Fried Cauliflower*

*Elderflower Ice Cream*

Pour oil into a wok or a high-sided frying pan, and add ginger and garlic. Infuse over a low heat for 5 minutes. Turn the heat up, and when it begins to sizzle, add the cauliflower. Stir-fry for 2 minutes, then add the sesame seeds. Continue to stir-fry for one more minute, then add sherry, soy sauce, sugar and 75 ml (2–3 fl oz) of water. Cover and leave to simmer for 5 minutes. Remove lid, turn heat to its highest, and cook until liquid has almost boiled away. Scatter with spring onion and serve.

# Cauliflower en Colère

I love this fiery way of cooking cauliflower – if you wish you can just break the chillies into large bits that can be fished out at the end of cooking, but I prefer to leave them in. The red flashes look so vivacious against the pale cauliflower, and anyway, if you are going to cook a hot peppery dish, then you might as well go the whole hog.

**SUGGESTED MENU**

*Avocado and Orange Salad*

*Baked Eggs on a Bed of Carrots and Leeks, with Cauliflower en Colère*

*Green Salad and Goat's Cheese*

*Fruit*

1 large cauliflower, cleaned and broken into small florets
45 ml (3 tablespoons) olive oil
1 clove of garlic, finely chopped
1 or 2 dried red chillies, crumbled
salt

team or boil cauliflower florets in salted water until just *al dente*. Drain well, and set aside until you are almost ready to eat.

Heat the olive oil gently with garlic and chilli. When hot, add cauliflower and sauté until lightly browned. Add salt if necessary.

## Cauliflower and Cashew Nut Soup

The combination of cauliflower and cashew nuts comes from a recipe for a cauliflower dish in Madhur Jaffrey's *Eastern Vegetarian Cooking*. It's a marvellous dish, and a marvellous combination. After eating it at a friend's house, I fell to thinking about other ways of exploiting this felicitous marriage. This soup was the best of the various results. Creamy and delicate and very soothing after a busy day.

| | |
|---|---|
| 1 medium-sized cauliflower, outer leaves removed, and broken into small florets | 15 ml (1 tablespoon) tahini |
| | 225 g (8 oz) natural yogurt |
| | salt |
| 1 onion, skinned and sliced | paprika |
| 25 g (1 oz) butter | fresh coriander leaves, or |
| 50 g (2 oz) cashew nuts | parsley, roughly chopped |
| 5 ml (1 teaspoon) sugar | |

immer cauliflower florets until soft. Drain, reserving cooking water. Soften the onion in half the butter over a medium heat. Sauté the cashew nuts until golden brown in the remaining butter.

Liquidise cauliflower, with cashew nuts, onion, and approximately 600 ml (1 pint) of cooking water. Pour into a large pan, and add sugar, tahini, yogurt, and salt and paprika to taste. Reheat gently, stirring occasionally, without actually boiling. It should be about the consistency of runny double cream, so dilute with more water if necessary. Serve, scattered with coriander or parsley, and an extra shake of red paprika to give colour.

# COURGETTES

I live in a third floor flat, quite gardenless except for a tiny balcony with just space enough for three large tubs. My past attempts at gardening have been spasmodic anyway, so maybe that's no bad thing. Nonetheless, I do, from time to time, yearn to be able to wander out of the back door and gather a few home-grown vegetables, flavour still untarnished by the normal lengthy journey from plant to shop and shop to customer.

This year my tubs have all been overflowing with herbs, but a couple of springs ago I was more adventurous and tenderly nursed tiny yellow courgette plants. Their flavour was superb. If you do grow them then it is worth picking them very young, and steaming them or stewing them for five minutes in butter or olive oil. They would be delicious used whole in the tempura recipe here.

**Edible blossoms** Courgette flowers are edible too but need to be used as soon as possible, before they wilt. In the South of France and Italy, you will find exuberant bunches of the egg-yolk yellow blossoms for sale in most summer markets. You're unlikely to find them here but if you do come across any, either turn them into crisp fritters (again the tempura batter below would work well) or stuff them loosely (the filling will expand), maybe with a rice based stuffing, and steam for 10 minutes. The *Shellfish Risotto*, shells all removed, on page 56 makes an elegant filling, and you would need only half quantities to fill more than a dozen flowers.

You could also use it, or most other risotto mixtures (for instance the *Risotto di Porcini* on page 112) to fill larger courgettes – halve lengthwise, scooping out a trench along the length of each half. Pack halves fairly tightly so that they don't roll over, cut-side up, in a heatproof dish. Fill each trench generously, dot with butter and steam or bake (but not if there's fish or shellfish in there), until courgettes are tender, but not collapsing. Serve as a first or main course, perhaps with a fresh tomato sauce.

Apart from simmering or steaming, one of the simplest ways to cook courgettes is to stew them sliced in olive oil or butter in a tightly-covered pan, with a small sprig of rosemary, or thyme, until soft and wickedly saturated with the butter or oil. I love them, too, *au gratin* – thinly sliced, and arranged in overlapping layers in an ovenproof dish. A generous trickle of olive oil over the top, salt and pepper and plenty of Parmesan, 20 minutes or so in a medium oven (exact temperature to depend on what else you're cooking), *et voilà*, the perfect combination of soft and crisp, vegetable and cheese and fruity olive oil. Below are three more major ways of cooking – the tempura recipe you will already be well aware of if you've read the preceding paragraphs, little nouvelle-ish eggy timbales, and a much heartier ragout with garlic and bacon.

## Vegetable Tempura

I have been told that in Japan the great test of a tempura chef is whether he can create the perfect 'tempura-ed' chrysanthemum leaf. The leaf must be only half-coated in batter, then fried at just the right temperature for a matter of seconds. The batter should be crisp, and the batter-free half still perfectly intact, not fried to a frazzle.

I'm not terribly keen on deep-frying on the whole – I love the final results, but it scares me rigid! There are times though, when I yearn for something crisp and light – the thought of these deep-fried vegetables in light tempura batter makes me determined to try.

If you don't have an electric deep-fryer, don't abandon hope – as long as you're well organised, and preferably have a willing hand to help set up an efficient production line, there should be no problems. The following quantities make an ample first course for six, or main course for three or four. If you wish to increase the quantities, add a dozen hard-boiled quails' eggs, some strips of firm fresh fish (e.g. monkfish, tuna, prawns, etc) and you can turn it into a superb main course. Just remember that someone is going to have to slave over the hot oil for twice as long!

A selection of 4 or 5 of the following: courgettes, green beans, mange-touts, tiny carrots, green, red or yellow peppers, fennel, cauliflower, pearl onions, or whatever looks freshest and youngest at the greengrocers. Allow, for instance, 4 small courgettes, 1 red and 1 yellow pepper, a dozen small carrots, and a large head of fennel.

SUGGESTED MENU

*Vegetable Tempura*
*Roast Chicken*
*with Two*
*Mushroom Sauce*
*Fruit and Nuts*

Tempura Batter:
2 small eggs
300 ml (½ pint) iced water
150 g (5 oz) plain flour
2.5 ml (½ teaspoon)
   bicarbonate of soda

extra flour
oil for frying
juice of 1 lemon, coarse salt
   and soy sauce to serve

Prepare the vegetables – halve, then quarter the courgettes lengthwise, top and tail the beans and mange-touts, scrape or peel carrots if necessary, seed the peppers and cut in strips, remove the outer layer of fennel and cut into thin rings, or strips, break the cauliflower into tiny florets, peel the onions (cover with boiling water for 30 seconds, and the skins should come off easily).

Beat the eggs, adding the iced water slowly. Tip sifted flour and bicarbonate of soda in at one fell swoop. Beat quickly, then set aside until you are ready to start frying. Don't worry about beating out any lumps – as long as they are not immense, they will actually improve the end product.

Set up your production line – prepared vegetables neatly laid out, next to them a plate of flour (and the bag nearby in case it runs out). Nearest to the deep-fryer, the bowl of batter. Have two serving dishes ready – both lined with kitchen paper to absorb any excess fat. Why two? Well, one is near the fryer, ready to receive the latest batch. The other is in the oven keeping the rest warm. Swap dishes every two or three batches and everything should stay crisp and hot.

Heat oil to about 180°C (350°F). Dust vegetables in flour (this will help the batter stick), dip in batter and fry for about two minutes in oil, until crisp and golden. Serve as quickly as possible before the batter has a chance to turn soggy, with a bowl of soy sauce, a bowl of lemon juice and a bowl of coarse salt, to dip vegetables into. Give everyone finger-bowls and plenty of napkins.

## Courgettes Paesana

This is a simple and most adaptable recipe – if you are baking other things at the same time, just shorten or lengthen the cooking time according to whether the oven temperature is higher or lower. Five or ten minutes more time in the oven will make little difference. I like to serve it from its cooking pot – the smell that invades the room as the lid is lifted is so evocative of the French countryside, warm suppers after long walks through golden autumnal landscape. Rustic romantic idylls. But a rather more elegant presentation in small bread cases has its attraction as well. It will serve six as a vegetable, or a first course, or four for a main course with the bread cases.

SUGGESTED MENU

*Tomato and Fennel Salad*

*Courgettes Paesana in Little Bread Cases*

*Zabaglione Coffee*

| | |
|---|---|
| 350 g (12 oz) courgettes, sliced into 1 cm (½ inch) discs | 6 cloves of garlic, skinned |
| | 2 glasses dry white wine |
| | 75 ml (5 tablespoons) olive oil |
| 175 g (6 oz) mushrooms, cleaned and quartered | 3 twigs fresh thyme, or 5 ml (1 teaspoon) dried |
| 5 rashers bacon, cut into thin strips | salt and freshly ground black pepper |
| 1 small onion, skinned and thinly sliced | finely chopped fresh parsley to serve |

Put all ingredients, except parsley, in an ovenproof casserole, stirring once to mix. Cover and bake at 180°C (350°F) gas mark 4 for 45–60 minutes. Scatter with fresh parsley.

**Bread cases**   Allow one brioche, or roll, per person for a first course dish, two for a main course. Cut a lid from each roll. Carefully scoop out the centre with a teaspoon, leaving a sturdy wall of bread. Brush inside and out with melted butter. Bake in a hot oven on a buttered baking tray for 15 minutes until crisp and golden.

# Timbales de Courgettes with Salsa Cruda

SUGGESTED MENU

*Timbales de Courgettes with Salsa Cruda*

*Grilled Cod with Anchovy and Orange Butter*

*Tropical Halva Cake*

These can be served as a first course with *Salsa Cruda* (see below), or maybe a richer hollandaise, or on their own as part of a selection of vegetables. You could also bake it in one large dish.

| | |
|---|---|
| 700 g (1½ lb) courgettes, thinly sliced | 50 g (2 oz) grated Gruyère |
| 90 ml (6 tablespoons) single cream | a few leaves of fresh basil, finely chopped, or a pinch of marjoram |
| 3 eggs | salt and freshly ground pepper |

Simmer courgettes until soft (about 5 minutes). Drain well and reserve 6 slices intact. Squeeze all excess water out of remaining courgettes. Mash coarsely with a potato masher or a fork. Add remaining ingredients and stir well.

Butter 6 small ramekins, or metal moulds, and place one of the reserved courgette slices in the centre of the base of each one. Fill each mould with courgette mixture. Pour enough hot water into a roasting pan to fill a depth of about 1 cm (½ inch). Stand moulds in the water and bake for 30–40 minutes at 200°C (400°F) gas mark 6 until just set. Remove from oven, and leave to stand for 4 or 5 minutes. Run a knife around the side of each one and turn out.

## Salsa Cruda

| | |
|---|---|
| 350 g (12 oz) ripe tomatoes, blanched, peeled, seeded and finely diced | 15 ml (1 tablespoon) finely chopped fresh basil, or a pinch of marjoram |
| 1 sweet red onion, skinned and finely chopped | salt and freshly ground pepper |
| olive oil | lemon juice, and sugar if necessary |

Combine tomato with onion and add oil, basil and seasonings to taste. If tomatoes are on the dull side add a squeeze of lemon juice, and a pinch or two of sugar. Chill.

If I had never eaten fennel before, and someone told me that it was a vegetable that tasted aniseedy, or even had a hint of liquorice to it, then my natural inclination would be to steer well clear of it. I never cared much for liquorice.

As a child, I tolerated the liquorice straws that led to the sherbet in a sherbet fountain. They soon got blocked anyway, and then the only thing to do was to yank them out and throw them away. I toyed occasionally with a liquorice allsort, because they always looked so pretty and colourful, and the pink and blue sugary bits diluted the black liquorice bands.

Other than that, liquorice has not cropped up in a big way in my life. But fennel is quite another matter. It is high on my list of preferred vegetables, with its beautiful pale greeny-white curves. It does have a taste that is akin to that of liquorice, but it is crisp, and juicy, fresh and subtle, not at all sticky and sickly sweet.

Fennel grew wild all over the French village I grew up in. There was a maze of paths and stairways that zig-zagged up and down the cliff, and the edges of these were dotted with the tall feathery plants. Wild fennel is not a fussy plant – drop a small branch accidentally on a patch of the poorest soil, and within days you will have the beginnings of a new plant, thrusting determinedly upwards.

**All purpose plant** We used the leaves and the seeds to flavour our food, and the dried stalks to fuel the barbecue when we cooked fish, but there was one delight the plant provided which had nothing whatsoever to do with our stomachs. It is the food plant of the caterpillar of the swallow-tail butterfly. Fully-grown, these elegant creatures would flutter and glide through the flowers of the garden, unperturbed by our presence.

The fleshy bulbous heads of fennel that we buy are the cultivated cousins of the wild plant. They are often known as Florentine fennel, to distinguish them from the herb. Traditionally fennel is served with or used as a flavouring for fish, but it is also delicious with chicken, pasta, rice, and cheese, especially Parmesan. It is wonderful cold and thinly sliced, in salads, but don't make the mistake I once did of thinking that, even colder, it might be used to create an unusual first course – fennel sorbet. It was quite disgusting, and I still shudder at the very thought of it.

Prepare fennel by chopping off the stalk stubs, and cutting a thin slice from the base. Ease off the outer layer, often damaged and dirty, and discard this along with the other bits and pieces. What remains is usually sliced thinly or quartered.

Fennel can be steamed or boiled until just tender, but it is also delicious stewed slowly, with a thinly-sliced onion and butter, or olive oil, in a covered pan. To make a fennel gratin, parboil or steam quartered fennel. Arrange in an ovenproof dish, sprinkle generously with Parmesan, or breadcrumbs mixed with Parmesan, dot with butter and bake in a medium hot oven until nicely browned.

Similarly, fennel can be baked with red mullet, or mackerel, say. Again cook fennel until just tender. Spread a thick layer in an ovenproof dish, and scatter with a few black olives. Embed the prepared fish in the fennel, dribble a little olive oil over the top and season. Bake in a medium hot oven until fish is just cooked through. Instead of fish, you might use chicken breasts, or tiny spring chickens – brown first in olive oil, or butter.

Fennel and tomato is a classic combination, either in a salad such as the one on page 127, or cooked. Arrange overlapping slices of half-cooked fennel and raw tomato in a gratin dish, sprinkle with grated cheese and olive oil, adding a few olives, perhaps, and bake until browned. Or serve cooked fennel in a thick tomato sauce (page 125), and again, you might finish it in the oven with breadcrumbs, or serve it poured over pasta.

Sticking with pasta for the minute, an even simpler but delicious dish is made by cutting a few heads of fennel into large chunks and cooking in a large pan of salted water. Cook pasta in the same water, keeping fennel hot, and then toss the two together with lots of butter and freshly ground pepper.

## Lemon Fennel Soup

SUGGESTED MENU

*Iced Lemon Fennel
Soup*

*Chicken Breasts en
Croûte*

*Gratin of Fresh
Pears*

This is a pale delicate soup that can be served hot or cold. The feathery green fennels fronds look charming against the green-white of the soup, and the lemon juice adds a subtle, but bright lift to the soup. Croûtons can be added as well as the parsley and lemon rind.

| | |
|---|---|
| 1 large onion, skinned and thinly sliced | salt and freshly ground black pepper |
| 50 g (2 oz) butter | grated rind and juice of 1 lemon |
| 2 large heads of fennel, thinly sliced, retaining feathery leaves. | 25 ml (1½ tablespoons) finely chopped parsley |
| 600–900 ml (1–1½ pints) milk | |

Soften the onion in three-quarters of the butter. Add the fennel slices, and stir until well coated with butter. Add 600 ml (1 pint) of milk and a pinch of salt, and bring to the boil. Simmer until fennel is soft. Liquidise until smooth, season and thin down with extra milk as desired.

To serve hot: When you are ready to eat, reheat the soup if necessary, and meanwhile, fry parsley and grated lemon rind quickly in remaining butter. Remove soup from heat, and stir in lemon juice to taste, and the fried parsley and lemon rind. Decorate with a few fronds of fennel leaves.

To serve cold: Stir in lemon juice to taste and chill. Just before serving, fry parsley and lemon rind as above, stir into soup and decorate with a few fronds of fennel.

# Fennel Risotto

This is a simple but very successful risotto. The flavour of the fennel is subtle, and melts into the buttery rice and piquant Parmesan. If you have any chicken stock, use that instead of water, then it will taste even better.

**SUGGESTED MENU**

*Grilled Pepper Salad with Olives and Eggs*

*Fennel Risotto with Mixed Salad*

*Poached Pears and Hot Chocolate Sauce*

3 large heads of fennel
75 g (3 oz) butter
1 onion, skinned and roughly chopped
350 g (12 oz) Arborio rice
1 glass dry white wine

salt and freshly ground black pepper
50 g (2 oz) grated Parmesan
45 ml (3 tablespoons) finely chopped parsley

Cut the woody stalks off the fennel, saving the wispy fronds. Discard the outer layer if necessary. Cut into small chunks. Melt the butter in a large pan, and soften the onion in it without browning.

Add the fennel, and the rice, and cook for a further 2 minutes, stirring to ensure that everything is well coated in butter. Add the white wine, and simmer until wine is absorbed.

Then add 150 ml (1/4 pint) of water (or stock), and simmer until that is absorbed. Repeat, until rice is soft. Stir in Parmesan, parsley, salt and pepper. Taste and adjust seasonings, and stir in an extra knob of butter, if you feel it needs it. Serve, with a few of the fennel fronds scattered over it.

## Fennel Siciliano

SUGGESTED MENU

*Crudités with
Goat's Cheese
Sauce*

*Fennel Siciliano*

*Strawberry and
Orange-Flower
Water Sorbet*

There are two ways of making this baked fennel dish. The first is much quicker – the fennel is just layered with the stuffing, and baked *au gratin*. It looks perfectly nice, but not nearly as pretty as when the fennel is actually stuffed with the stuffing. If you have time, use the second method.

When the fennel is incorporated into the stuffing, as in the second method, it can be used instead to stuff a whole chicken, scooped-out tomatoes, or even peppers or aubergines.

6 large heads of fennel
50 g (2 oz) butter plus extra
   for greasing
100 g (4 oz) breadcrumbs
25 g (1 oz) pine kernels
50 g (2 oz) raisins
5 ml (1 teaspoon) dried
   thyme or 2 sprigs fresh
   thyme

6 anchovy fillets, finely
   chopped
40 g (1½ oz) freshly grated
   Parmesan
salt and freshly ground black
   pepper

Method 1 (quicker): Cut off stalks and discard outer layers of fennel bulbs if necessary. Slice thinly. Simmer in salted water until just soft, and drain well.

Melt the butter. Mix remaining ingredients together, and add the butter. Grease a gratin dish, and lay the fennel slices in it in an even layer. Spread the breadcrumb mixture over the top, and bake at 190°C (375°F) gas mark 5 for 30–40 minutes until nicely browned.

Method 2 (prettier): Cut stalks off and discard the outer layer of the fennel bulbs if necessary. Cut a thin slice from the base of a bulb, and gently ease off the next layer, keeping it intact. Do the same with the second layer, and fit the two back together, to form a cylinder. Repeat with the other bulbs.

Finely dice 4 of the hearts of the fennel, and save the other 2 for next day. Put the diced fennel in a pan with the butter, and cover. Stew over a low heat for 10–15 minutes until fennel is soft. Meanwhile, bring a large pan of salted water to the boil and par-boil the fennel cylinders for 4 minutes. Drain well, and secure cylinders with cocktail sticks. Place close together on an ovenproof dish.

Mix diced fennel and buttery juices with remaining ingredients, and fill the cylinders. Scatter any extra stuffing around the fennel. Bake at 190°C (375°F) gas mark 5 for 30 minutes, until stuffing is beginning to brown.

## Hot Fennel and Potato Salad

I'm rather partial to the hot Germanic potato salads, and the combination of fennel and potato in this version works particularly well. Serve it with grilled sausages – *bratwurst*, French *boudin blanc*, garlic sausage, or really good high-meat content English sausages – or the smoked rings of boiling sausage.

It would also go well with one of the sturdier kinds of fish, such as grilled or baked tuna or swordfish steaks.

**SUGGESTED MENU**

*Crudités with Pesto and Tofu Sauce*

*Hot Potato and Fennel Salad with Grilled Bratwurst*

*Fichi di Sardegna*

450 g (1 lb) new potatoes, scrubbed
2 heads of fennel
60 ml (4 tablespoons) olive oil
15 ml (1 tablespoon) wine vinegar

5–10 ml (1–2 teaspoons) Dijon mustard
salt and freshly ground black pepper

**S**team or boil the potatoes. Leave to cool, then peel. Cut the stalks off the fennel, saving the wispy green fronds. Discard the outer layer if necessary. Cut the fennel into large chunks, and steam or boil for 5 minutes.

In a large frying pan – or two frying pans may be easier – sauté the fennel in 15 ml (1 tablespoon) of oil, for a few minutes until beginning to brown. Keep warm in the oven, and add the remaining oil to the pan. Sauté the potatoes. Add potatoes to fennel.

Take the pan off the heat, and pour in vinegar – take care as it may spit. If it is a cast-iron pan that retains the heat well, let it cool for a couple of minutes first. Stir in the mustard, salt and pepper, then pour over potatoes and fennel. Taste and adjust seasonings. Serve scattered with some of the fennel fronds.

## Other FENNEL Recipes

**Tomato and Fennel Salad** *(page 127)*
**Crudités** *(page 40)*

# LETTUCES AND OTHER SALAD LEAVES

In France, a meal without a good green salad, served after the main course, is no meal at all. I'm occasionally prepared to break tradition and take my lettuce with my main course, but on the whole I'm inclined to agree. Nutritionally speaking, there is little to be said in the lettuce's favour, or against it for that matter. True the Flopsy Bunnies fell fast asleep after eating too much bolted lettuce, and in large quantities some kinds do apparently have a hallucinogenic effect, but you would have to eat an awful lot of greenery before it began to have the slightest effect upon you.

No, the importance of a green salad is not because it is good for you, nor for that matter is it tempting because it is bad for you. It is merely this: a good green salad is very nice indeed. It provides a gentle breathing space between courses, and cleanses and refreshes the palate, without lying heavy in the stomach.

So what constitutes a 'good green salad'? For a start, not the floppy tasteless leaves of the most widely available lettuce, the bland round lettuce. That has two uses only – one as a way of wrapping up little food parcels, as in the recipe for *Plaice Fillets Wrapped in Lettuce* (see page 47), and the other for making soup, or adding moisture to stews. Otherwise forget it. The first and most important thing is to choose a leaf with texture, body and flavour. The second is to create a decent dressing for it. And the third is to combine the two at the table and not before.

Choose a healthy-looking lettuce for a start. The outside leaves may be ripped or nibbled, or muddy, but the inner leaves should be lively and bouncy. Eat it on the day of purchase, or at least within a couple of days. Place the whole lettuce in a plastic bag, sprinkle with a few drops of water and seal, and leave it in the bottom of the fridge. Clean it up only an hour or two before it is to be eaten. Once you've washed and dried the leaves (roll them in a clean tea towel, or pat dry with kitchen paper, or swing them vigorously in a wire basket), put them into a clean plastic bag, seal and return to the fridge, until ready to assemble the salad.

Make the dressing, and pour into the salad bowl. Put the salad servers into the bowl, so that they will support the lettuce and keep it away from the dressing until the moment it is tossed. When you've reached the salad stage of the meal, heap the lettuce on top of the servers, and take it through to the table. Toss it, then eat it.

## The Leaf

If all else fails, go for an Iceberg lettuce. Crisp, crunchy and juicy, but not a winner on the flavour stakes. With a good lively dressing – the Moroccan orange juice dressing (see page 166) is a winner with the Iceberg – it will fit the bill.

**Chinese leaf** or **cabbage** is wonderfully juicy too, and has a more pronounced rather sweet flavour. Again, an orange juice dressing goes well, or one made with sesame oil, or with a dash of soy sauce. A plain French dressing, made perhaps with sherry or balsamic vinegar, would not go amiss either.

**Webb's Wonder** and **Cos** are two first rate lettuces, that make excellent salads dressed with a French dressing, in particular one made with a walnut or hazelnut oil, together with matching croûtons or nuts. Add lots of fragrant herbs perhaps, garlic, or finely chopped spring onion, or sweet red onion. Serve a ripe Camembert at the same time, as the French often do.

**Spinach** salads are becoming very popular. Choose lively unblemished young leaves, wash thoroughly, and toss with strips of bacon, or crumbled goat's cheese, and a French dressing, possibly garlicky.

**Frisée** or **Curly Endive** is one of my favourite salad leaves, with its strong, bitter edge. Personally, I love it on its own dressed with a classic French dressing, and any of the additions that go with a Cos lettuce. Together with the oak leaf lettuce, it is the prettiest of lettuces, wispy and delicate, varying in colour from the yellow of its centre to the bright spring green of its outer leaves. I often add a sprinkling of small-diced tomato to it – not so much for taste, but because it makes such a cheerful sight. But some people find it on the strong side and prefer to mix it with other leaves.

The **Oak Leaf lettuce** or **Feuilles de Chêne**, sometimes bronzed, dark red in colour, sometimes green, is very easy to recognise. The name says it all. It tastes and looks good, though with a less pronounced flavour than the Frisée. Use it on its own, as one would a Cos or Webb's, or as part of a mixed green salad.

The dark magenta red curls of **Radicchio**, or **Red Chicory**, are also easily recognisable. They have a delicious but quite pronounced bitter taste, and even I agree that they are best mixed with other leaves.

**Mâche** also known as **Lamb's Lettuce** or **Corn Salad** is a small, tongue-shaped leaf, with an almost velvety surface. I used to pick it wild on the rock walls around our garden in France, and it took forever to collect enough for one decent-sized salad. The cultivated Mâche is larger and comes ready-picked. It's pretty, and nicely flavoured. Dress with a dressing made from a flavoured wine vinegar. Scatter with fine diced tomato. It is a good addition to a mixed leaf salad.

## Dressings

There are specific recipes for vinaigrettes and dressings scattered throughout the book. This is just a quick summary. First of all, don't be tempted to use a thick creamy dressing on a green salad. It looks dreadful, and regardless of what it tastes like, that's enough to dampen most people's interest. Stick with the oil-based dressings, or substitute a good chicken stock for part or all of the oil, if you are intent on cutting down calories.

The universal **French Dressing** is open to hundreds of variations. For a basic French dressing, I use a ratio of 4 tablespoons of oil to 1 tablespoon of white wine vinegar, $1/2$ teaspoon French mustard, with a pinch of sugar, salt and freshly ground black pepper. It is now easy to buy not just red and white wine vinegar, but vinegars flavoured with herbs, or fruit (raspberry has been very fashionable over here, and blueberry equally popular in America), or spices. There is also the wonderful rich-tasting sherry vinegar, or the perfumed balsamic wine vinegar.

Now easily available too, are a whole panoply of oils. As well as a confusing choice of olive oils – use a fruity one, of middle weight and colour, for salads – many nut oils are now available. Walnut and hazelnut oil may seem expensive, but they are strong. Use half and half with a tasteless oil, such as grapeseed. Some Chinese groundnut or peanut oils do not have the taste refined out of them, and are worth trying. The darker sesame oils are delicious too. Fry a few cubes of bread in the same oil, and toss into the salad at the last minute.

The Italian or Greek **Lemon and Olive Oil Dressing** is similar to a French dressing. Mix lemon juice with oil in a proportion of 1 to 3 or 4, and season with salt, pepper, and maybe a pinch of sugar. Herbs such as basil, or chives, thyme, marjoram, oregano, or rigani can be added. Use with a Greek salad (shredded lettuce, tomato, cucumber, sweet onion, and crumbled feta cheese), or when you want a very clear, pure taste.

To add a hint of garlic to a salad, wipe the bowl with the cut side of a halved garlic clove. Actually, I find this a bit niggardly – if you want garlic, then use garlic! Stronger, without actually indulging in whole bits (though there's nothing wrong with that either, in my opinion) is an oil infused with garlic. Either add a couple of halved cloves of garlic to a small jar of olive oil, and leave for a couple of days, or heat the oil gently with the garlic, then cover and leave to infuse for half an hour or so.

To make a **Hot Bacon Dressing**, cut four or five rashers of streaky bacon into strips and fry in 30 ml (2 tablespoons) of oil. When golden brown, pour bacon and oil over the salad. Add 30 ml (2 tablespoons) of wine vinegar to the frying pan, and when it bubbles, add that to the salad too. Season, and serve quickly, whilst the lettuce still has some life left in it. Be careful not to overcook the bacon, and if you use a cast-iron frying pan, let it cool for a minute or so before adding the vinegar. I've sometimes ended up with an unpleasant burnt and bitter dressing.

Dressings made with orange juice can be very refreshing. Try the Moroccan orange juice and orange-flower dressing on page 166. It goes well with lightly-flavoured lettuces, such as the Iceberg, or Chinese leaf. On page 76 is another orange dressing that uses either the juice of a Seville orange, or a mixture of orange and lemon juice. It is more boisterous than the Moroccan dressing, and won't be drowned by some of the more domineering lettuces.

Lovely peppery **watercress** goes with most things. Wash it well, and cut or tear it up into smallish pieces. Sprawling branches of watercress that take over the entire plate can be tiresome and off-putting. Save large stalks for soup making. The best way I've found of making watercress last, is to keep it upside down in a bowl of water in the fridge, so that the leaves are constantly bathed in cool water. Serve it on its own, with an orange, or lemon or French dressing. Use a good olive oil, but don't bother with the expensive nut oils.

If you grow it, or can get hold of it, treat **sorrel** as a herb in salads. Its taste is so sharp, that a single leaf, finely chopped or shredded will make a big impact.

Make the most of your weeds – blanch young dandelion leaves (that haven't yet been sprayed with weed killer, or any other offensive or dangerous substances), by covering the plant with a flower pot, and leaving it there for a couple of weeks or more. This reduces the natural bitterness. Wash well, and serve with a bacon dressing.

If you are making a mixed leaf salad, pick out three leaves that contrast in taste, and in form, that is if you have the choice. A good mixture, for instance, might be bronzed Oak Leaf lettuce, Mâche, and Frisée. Keep the dressing simple, but use the best quality oils and wine or sherry vinegars. Add herbs, garlic, and/or finely chopped sweet or spring onion, or shallots.

Not leaves at all, **nasturtium** and **chive** flowers can both be added to salads, and look enchantingly pretty. Nasturtium flowers are increasingly to be found on sale in supermarkets packaged and ready for use in a salad.

# SWEET PEPPERS

It's funny to think that forty or so years ago, the common bell pepper was almost unknown in Northern Europe. Now every shop with the slightest pretensions towards greengrocery, stocks amidst the limp lettuces, the squashy tomatoes and wrinkling cucumbers, at least a few weary green peppers, and a couple of sorry-looking red ones. How much better, though, when you catch sight of a high mound of shining, cheerful peppers, skin stretched tight and smooth.

Peppers, like tomatoes, are fruits of the sun and sitting in a bowl on the kitchen table, they are a happy reminder of the vibrant, noisy markets of the Mediterranean.

Of the open air market in Nice, for instance, where they sell big bundles of wild thyme, oregano, and dry fennel stalks, over which fish is grilled. Bright orange bunches of courgette flowers, for fritters or stuffing – wide-eyed and lively in the morning, already closed and wilting by early afternoon. Wild mushrooms in profusion, huge craggy tomatoes, shining aubergines, artichokes and fennel bulbs, purple figs, green figs, and more and more and more. And in all that bustle and banter, there are purple, and horn-shaped pale green peppers, as well as red and green and yellow.

**Crudités**   Never be tempted by cut-price peppers that are damaged, or wrinkled and past their prime. These are obviously useless for using raw as they will have lost their crisp juiciness, and sweetness, and will collapse if cooked, giving a dull taste. Crudités, crisp raw vegetables, served with a bowl of French dressing, or other sauce, maybe just mayonnaise, or soured cream, or a collection of sauces, are unquestionably a good way to start a meal, and I always include peppers – sometimes just green ones, when I am sticking religiously to green vegetables: fennel, celery, spring onions, cucumber, parboiled French beans, mange-touts, and so on.

The sensuous, Mediterranean grilled pepper salad, is proof, if needed, that simplicity is often best in cooking. Prepare peppers under the grill or in the oven as in *Three Pepper Soufflé* (page 108) or *Pepper and Ricotta Parcels* (page 109), taking care to lose as little of the juice as possible. Cut into long, wide strips, and turn in French dressing or an olive oil and lemon dressing while still warm, then serve at room temperature with lots of parsley, or basil. Strips of anchovy go well with this salad, or can be mashed into the dressing.

Peperonata is a vegetable stew that lies somewhere between a standard tomato sauce, and a ratatouille. To make it, follow the recipe for *Tomato Sauce* on page 125, but halve the quantity of tomatoes, and add two red peppers and a yellow pepper (or three red peppers), cut into strips, to the frying onions. Fry gently for a few minutes before adding the tomatoes. Stew until all wateriness has disappeared, and flavour with basil. Eat it hot, warm, or cool.

One step more, and you end up with piperade – when peperonata is cooked, add six beaten eggs, and stir over a low heat as if making scrambled eggs, removing from the heat as soon as it is thick and creamy. Meanwhile, heat six thick slices of good ham in butter in a frying pan (or in the oven, piled up and dotted with butter). Fill each slice, like a pancake, with the egg and pepper mixture, and serve hot.

# Crudités with Pesto and Tofu Sauce

My ideal summer menu might well begin with a dish of crudités with aioli – garlic mayonnaise. The sweetness of raw vegetables – yellow and red peppers particularly – goes so well with the silky smoothness of real mayonnaise, over-indulgent oiliness fought off by the punch of raw garlic.

This, though, is an equally good, but less oily sauce made with tofu (bean curd). Be sure to buy silken tofu, rather than the ordinary kind – healthfood shops usually stock both. Silken tofu comes in a block, but is much softer and better suited to sauce making. Use home-made pesto ideally, or a good make of the greenest bought pesto. As with aioli, I usually make this sauce the day before – an overnight rest in the fridge mellows the flavour – but this isn't absolutely necessary. It is, after all, an excellent emergency sauce, that can be run up in a matter of minutes, from ingredients that all keep well.

**SUGGESTED MENU**

*Crudités with Pesto and Tofu Sauce*

*Tandoori Chicken Kebabs with Rice*

*Moroccan Orange and Mooli Salad*

*Potted Stilton with Peppered Pears*

A selection of sweet young vegetables, including plenty of fresh peppers – green, red, yellow, and if you are lucky enough to see them, the rarer dark purple-black peppers. See recipe for Goat's Cheese Sauce on page 40 for more suggestions.

275 g (10 oz) silken tofu
30 ml (2 tablespoons) pesto
1 clove of garlic, skinned
30 ml (2 tablespoons) fruity olive oil
freshly ground black pepper and salt
a few leaves of basil or parsley

Prepare the vegetables as in recipe for *Crudités with Goat's Cheese Sauce* on page 40. Drain the tofu. Liquidise with all the other ingredients, except basil, until smooth. Taste and adjust seasonings. Serve chilled, decorated with a few leaves of basil or parsley, and surrounded by prepared vegetables.

If you don't have a liquidiser, mash the tofu with a fork, then beat in the remaining ingredients.

## Three Pepper Soufflé

SUGGESTED MENU

*Smoked Chicken and Pear Salad*

*Three Pepper Soufflé with a Tomato Salad, or Green Salad, and Steamed Buttered New Potatoes*

*Iced Mango and Cardamom Fool*

Soufflés have always been one of my great standbys. As a student, I impressed friends – well, male friends, anyway – by quickly whipping up a cheese soufflé for supper. I never did understand why they seemed quite so impressed – soufflés are easy to make.

This is just a variation on the ordinary cheese soufflé, but the Parmesan and the peppers combine to give it a special flavour. Always use freshly grated Parmesan. The pre-packaged grated Parmesan tastes like sawdust in comparison. Either make this in two 15-cm (6-inch) soufflé dishes, or in a large oval gratin dish – I use one that is about 33 cm (13 inches) long, by 23 cm (9 inches) wide.

A year or two ago, I made a marvellous discovery about soufflés. Prue Leith in her three-volume *Cookery Course* insists that soufflés can be frozen uncooked, whites and all, and cooked straight from the freezer. She's right. Turn your freezer to its coldest setting, and whip soufflés straight into it as soon as you have folded in the egg whites, and poured into the dishes. Add 5 minutes on to the cooking time.

---

| | |
|---|---|
| 1 red pepper, quartered and seeded | 50 g (2 oz) butter |
| 1 yellow pepper (or a second red pepper), quartered and seeded | 50 g (2 oz) flour |
| | 600 ml (1 pint) milk |
| | 50 g (2 oz) finely grated Parmesan |
| 1 green pepper, quartered and seeded | freshly ground black pepper |
| 6 rashers smoked back bacon, rinded and cut into strips | 6 egg yolks |
| | salt |
| | 8 egg whites |

---

Grill the pieces of pepper, skin side up, under a very hot grill, until blackened and blistered. Pop into a plastic bag, and seal. Leave until cool enough to handle easily. Peel off blackened skin, and dice.

Dry fry the bacon, in a non-stick pan, until beginning to brown. Melt butter in a medium-sized pan, and stir in flour. Cook for a minute, then add milk little by little to make a white sauce. Simmer for 10 minutes, then off the heat, add Parmesan, and the ground pepper. Stir until Parmesan is melted, then add grilled peppers, and bacon. Finally add egg yolks. Taste, and adjust seasonings, adding salt if necessary. It should be on the strong side, as we have yet to add the egg whites.

Beat the egg whites until stiff, and fold into cheese and pepper sauce. Pour into dish(es), and bake for 18–22 minutes at 200°C (400°F) gas mark 6. The soufflé should be browned and well risen, with its centre still slightly runny. Serve immediately.

## Pepper and Ricotta Parcels

Cut into these puff pastry parcels, and you get the prettiest stripy cross section. They can be served as a first course, or double the quantities to make a vegetarian main course that should satisfy meat-eaters as well. I would serve them sauceless, but you might like to add a tomato sauce, or maybe just a small pool of melted butter, flavoured with herbs.

**SUGGESTED MENU**

*Poisson Cru Niçois*
*Pepper and Ricotta
Parcels*
*Fichi di Sardegna*

1 red pepper
1 yellow pepper (or a second
  red pepper)
1 green pepper
350 g (12 oz) ricotta
40 g (1½ oz) freshly grated
  Parmesan
15 ml (1 tablespoon) chopped
  fresh parsley
15 ml (1 tablespoon) chopped
  fresh mint
15 ml (1 tablespoon) chopped
  fresh basil, or marjoram
If you can't get these,
  substitute other fresh
  herbs, such as chives,
  chervil, thyme or rosemary
  in moderation
freshly ground black pepper
250 g (9 oz) puff pastry
flour
1 egg, beaten

Bake the three peppers in a hot oven – around 220°C (425°F) gas mark 7 – until blackened and blistered. This should take about 20 minutes. Pop them quickly into a plastic bag and seal. Leave until they are cool enough to handle.

Beat the ricotta with Parmesan, herbs and pepper. Divide into 12 portions. As soon as they are cool, remove peppers (which will have collapsed and turned floppy) from the bag, and strip off skin. Halve each pepper and discard stalk and seeds. Divide each half into thirds. Take a piece of yellow pepper, and spread it with one portion of the ricotta mixture. Cover this with a piece of green pepper, and spread with another portion of the ricotta, and finally top with a piece of red pepper. Repeat with remaining pieces of pepper, and ricotta.

Divide pasty into thirds. Roll out one third, on a floured board, into a large rectangle. Halve the rectangle, and use each piece to wrap one of the pepper and ricotta piles, brushing edges with beaten egg and pressing to seal firmly. Place on a baking tray, with edges tucked neatly underneath. Brush with beaten egg. Repeat with remaining pastry.

Bake at 220°C (425°F) gas mark 7 for 15 minutes until puffed and brown. Serve hot.

# DRIED PORCINI

*Porcini* means two things in Italian, little pigs, piglets, and more importantly in this case, ceps, *boletus edulis*, one of the finest of mushrooms. They are used fresh in the early autumn, and dried or bottled for use throughout the year. Most Italian delicatessens stock dried porcini. They are usually packaged in minuscule amounts, but the strong, meaty flavour goes a long way.

For most of us, it's not so easy to lay our hands on a regular supply of fresh ceps. Occasionally, one finds them for sale at great expense in smart shops, but usually one must make do with the dried variety. I always keep a couple of packets in the cupboard as a standby. Some shops sell them loose from large jars, but I find the quality variable. They lose some of their strength from frequent exposure to the air.

To prepare dried porcini for cooking, you must first soak them in hot water, for at least half an hour. Don't throw the water away once you've drained the porcini, as you would be pouring good vegetable stock down the drain. Either save it, and use it to add extra flavour to soups or sauces, or incorporate it in the dish you are cooking. Before use, strain it through a sieve lined with a piece of muslin to remove any fine grit. To make a simple sauce for pasta, slice the soaked porcini, then stew in butter or olive oil for five minutes. Onions and garlic can be added – cook them first in the butter. Finally, pour in the soaking water, and simmer until it has almost completely evaporated. Add salt and pepper, and toss into the cooked pasta with plenty of fresh parsley. Serve with or without Parmesan.

## Two Mushroom Sauce

**SUGGESTED MENU**

*Vegetable Tempura*
*Roast Chicken*
*Stuffed with ¼*
*quantity of Risotto*
*di Porcini with*
*Two Mushroom*
*Sauce*
*Fruit and Nuts*

This is a rich mushroom sauce, made with common or garden commercial button mushrooms, impregnated with the strong flavour of the porcini. Serve it with pasta, with grilled, baked or poached fish, or grilled or roast chicken.

1 10-g (¹/₂-oz) packet porcini
1 onion, skinned and sliced
1 clove of garlic, skinned
and finely chopped
350 g (12 oz) button
mushrooms, cleaned and
finely chopped

50 g (2 oz) butter
150 ml (¹/₄ pint) double
cream
salt, freshly ground black
pepper
30 ml (2 tablespoons) finely
chopped parsley

Cover porcini with boiling water, and leave to soak for at least 30 minutes. Drain, pat dry and slice. Strain soaking water and reserve.

Fry onion and garlic in butter until soft, but without browning. Add porcini, and their soaking water. Simmer until water has completely evaporated. Add chopped fresh mushrooms, salt and pepper. Cover pan and stew for 20 minutes. Uncover and raise heat. Cook until liquid has almost evaporated. Add cream, and simmer for a further 5 minutes. Taste, and adjust seasonings. Stir in parsley, and serve.

## Risotto di Porcini

As with all risottos, it is important that you use proper Italian risotto rice. *Arborio* is one of the best and the easiest to find. Other suitable types are *carnaroli*, or *vialone.* These all absorb a lot of liquid, without becoming mushy, to give the correct moist consistency of a perfect risotto. I prefer to use a medium dry, or even a sweet white wine for this recipe, but a dry white, especially if it is the one you intend to drink with it, would be fine.

SUGGESTED MENU

*Risotto di Porcini*
*Mixed Leaf Salad*
*Coconut Crème*
*Brûlée*

3 x 10-g (½-oz) packets
  porcini
100 g (4 oz) butter
2 medium-sized onions,
  skinned and chopped
2 cloves of garlic, skinned
  and chopped
450 g (1 lb) Arborio rice

300 ml (½ pint) white wine
salt and freshly ground black
  pepper
75–100 g (3–4 oz) freshly
  grated Parmesan
30 ml (2 tablespoons) freshly
  chopped parsley

Pour hot water over the porcini, and leave to soak for half an hour. Drain, and chop mushrooms. Strain soaking water to remove any grit, and reserve.

Melt half the butter in a heavy-bottomed pan, and soften onion and garlic, without browning. Add the mushrooms and rice, and stir for 2 minutes, to absorb the butter. Add the soaking water, a small pinch of salt, pepper and the white wine. Simmer until liquid is nearly all absorbed. Add 300 ml (½ pint) of hot water, and again simmer until almost completely absorbed, stirring frequently. Repeat this with more hot water, adding just 150 ml (¼ pint) at a time until rice is just cooked, but still with some bite. The amount of water required will vary from one packet of rice to another, but reckon on adding about 1 litre (1¾ pints). The whole process should take about 20 minutes.

Stir in the remaining butter, Parmesan and parsley. Taste and adjust seasonings, and serve as quickly as possible.

# Aubergine Parmigiana with Porcini

Usually, this dish is cooked without the porcini, but I find that they turn it into the perfect main course for a dinner where some of the eaters are vegetarian, and others are keen carnivores. Steaming, instead of frying, the aubergine slices, not only makes it less fatty, but also cuts down on preparation time.

| | |
|---|---|
| **2 x 10-g (1/2-oz) packet porcini** | **75 g (3 oz) freshly grated Parmesan** |
| **1.1 kg (21/2 lb) aubergines** | **225 g (8 oz) mozzarella** |
| **15 ml (1 tablespoon) olive oil** | **freshly ground black pepper** |
| **600 ml (1 pint) thick Tomato Sauce (see page 125)** | |

Cover porcini with hot water and leave to soak for half an hour. Remove stalks, and slice aubergines lengthways, or across, but they should be about 1 cm (1/2 inch) thick. Steam in a single layer, until soft.

Drain mushrooms, and slice. Strain soaking water to remove grit and reserve. Melt butter in a small pan, and add mushrooms. Fry gently for 3 minutes, then add the soaking water. Simmer until liquid is almost all evaporated. Coat the base of a large ovenproof dish, about 5 cm (2 inches) deep, with tomato sauce. On this, lay a layer of aubergines, then a layer of mozzarella and mushrooms. Sprinkle with pepper and Parmesan. Repeat until you have used up all the aubergine and mozzarella and porcini, ending up with a layer of aubergine. Dribble over any remaining tomato sauce, sprinkle with the last of the Parmesan, and finally trickle extra olive oil over the top of it all.

If after all that, you still have time, bake for 50–60 minutes at around 160°C (325°F) gas mark 3, until browned and bubbling. It can also be cooked at a higher temperature, say 200°C (400°F) gas mark 6, and will take 30 minutes or so. It does benefit from the longer, slower cooking, but it's an adaptable recipe, so adjust cooking time to suit your situation.

## Spaghetti Carbonara con Porcini

Spaghetti Carbonara has always been one of my favourite pasta dishes. It is, as well, a perfect emergency dish, that can be thrown together in a few minutes. In the standard version, *pancetta*, or bacon, is used, not porcini. Preferably the smoked *pancetta*, available from good Italian shops. Sometimes a few tablespoons of cream are also added, but I think it just as good without. In either case, the eggy sauce should thicken in the heat of the pasta and the oil, but it should not coagulate. Have the egg mixture and the porcini ready and easily to hand, as the pasta reaches the *al dente* stage, then move fast to combine all three. Do not feel tempted to replace pan over the heat once you have done this – you might spoil the whole dish.

> **SUGGESTED MENU**
>
> *Parma Ham with Exotic Fruit*
>
> *Spaghetti Carbonara con Porcini*
>
> *Mixed Leaf Salad*
>
> *Chocolate and Cointreau-Coated Strawberries*

2 x 10-g (½-oz) packets of porcini
60 ml (4 tablespoons) olive oil
4 eggs

salt and freshly ground black pepper
75 g (3 oz) grated Parmesan
400 g (14 oz) spaghetti
freshly chopped parsley to serve

**C**over porcini with hot water, and leave to soak for half an hour. Reserve the soaking liquid, drain and chop. Strain the soaking liquid to remove grit, and reserve. Beat eggs with pepper and Parmesan.

Heat 15 ml (a tablespoon) of oil in a small frying pan, and add porcini. Fry for 2 or 3 minutes, then add the cooking water. Simmer until water is evaporated, then add remaining oil, and heat thoroughly. Cook the spaghetti in plenty of boiling salted water. If it is fresh, it will need only a few minutes, so start the sauce first. If dried it will take longer and you can prepare the mushrooms whilst it is cooking.

As soon as spaghetti is *al dente*, drain well, and return to pan. Pour mushrooms and hot oil over it, and then add egg mixture. Toss quickly, and serve sprinkled with parsley, and with extra Parmesan for those who want it.

A friend's mother, now living in Derry in Northern  **POTATOES**
Ireland remembers her uncle telling her about the old rural way of eating potatoes: 'praties and dab at a stool'. Around the turn of the century, in agricultural Ulster, the two-person stool was a common item of furniture in farmhouses. On either side of the stool, were two smooth hollows, there by design, or worn away by the passage of hundreds of behinds. Like the kitchen table these stools were rigorously and regularly scrubbed clean.

On a cold evening, the stool would be pulled up to the fire by the man of the family. Sitting astride the stool, bottom firmly settled in one of the hollows, he waited for the companion hollow to be piled up with hot potatoes, boiled in their jackets. On the bridge that divided the two hollows, he poured a pile of salt, and then one by one he picked the potatoes off the pile, dipped them in the salt, and filled his belly – 'praties and dab at a stool'.

Nowadays, potatoes no longer hold the position of importance in Ireland that they once did, but they are still an essential part of the diet. Quality is fervently discussed and debated. To call a potato a 'ball of flour', is a high and very specific compliment. Far from implying a floury crumbly potato, it refers to one that melts in the mouth – so it might well be applied to one of the waxier types.

But around the area of London in which I live, despite the relatively large Irish population, there is little variety when it comes to potatoes. We are offered three or maybe four sorts, Maris Piper (floury), King Edward (floury), Desirée (less floury) and usually indiscriminate new (the best bet). The firm waxy potatoes, that make the best salads, and the best boiled potatoes, are a rare treat.

**Mashed potatoes**  All those floury potatoes are ideal for making mashed potatoes. Ideally bake the potatoes, to get a good dry base. Add cream, lots of butter or eggs when mashing. In Ireland, 'champ' or 'poundies' is a variation of the basic mash, with the addition of lots of finely chopped spring onions. In France, mashed potatoes are mixed with cream, garlic and grated Emmenthal, to make Aligot. Caraway seeds, finely chopped green chilli, yogurt, coriander leaves, parsley, chives and other herbs, might also be added to creamy mashed potato.

Sautéed potatoes are delicious, but require last-minute attention in the kitchen. If you have been cooking a duck, strain the fat through a muslin-lined sieve, then use to sauté with next day. Add herbs such as rosemary, or tarragon, dill weed or seed towards the end of cooking, for extra pzazz. Home-made crisps are easy if you have an electric deep-fryer, and a great improvement on the bought variety. Slice the peeled potato very thinly with a mandolin cutter. Then deep-fry quickly at 190°C (375°F). Similarly, those crisp little matchstick potatoes, that go so well with game, are best made at home – cut the potatoes into julienne strips and fry at 190°C (375°F) until golden.

Potato gratins are all made and cooked in the same manner as the *Jansson's Temptation* or *Smoked Salmon Gratin* below. To make Pommes Anna, wipe the dish thoroughly with a halved clove of garlic, and dot each layer of potato with lots of butter, salt and pepper. Pommes Boulangère is alternate layers of thinly sliced potato and onion, moistened with chicken stock and butter. For a Gratin Savoyard, add grated Gruyère and thinly sliced garlic, then moisten with half water (or stock), half wine. Finally Gratin Dauphinois is a controversial dish. Some people swear that it should be made with just a hint of garlic, milk, and double cream mixed with a teaspoon of flour to prevent separation. But there are many supporters of the alternative version, with added cheese, and an egg beaten into the cream and milk. Both are delicious, so take your pick.

## Stoved Potatoes with Pearl Onions or Garlic

Stoved new potatoes, cooked long and slow in a little butter, with a sprinkling of coarse sea salt, take on a special nutty taste that you won't get by cooking them any other way. Larger potatoes can be used instead – peel first and quarter. Little pearl onions, or cloves of garlic, benefit from this method of cooking as well, and combined with potatoes, make a delicious vegetable stew.

450 g (1 lb) new potatoes
    and 450 g (1 lb) pearl
    onions
or 700 g (1½ lb) new potatoes
    and 1 whole head of garlic

30 ml (2 tablespoons) water
50 g (2 oz) butter
15 ml (1 tablespoon) coarse
    sea salt

**SUGGESTED MENU**

*Chicken Livers with Almond and Garlic Sauce*

*Aubergine Parmigiana with Porcini, Stoved Potatoes with Pearl Onions*

*Elderflower Sorbet*

Scrub the potatoes. If you are using the pearl onions, top and tail, cover with boiling water and leave for 30 seconds. Drain, and skin. If you are using garlic, separate the cloves, and peel.

Put the potatoes and the onions or garlic in a large heavy pan that has a close-fitting lid. Add the water, and dot with the butter. Sprinkle with coarse sea salt, and cover. Place over a low heat, and leave to stew slowly for an hour or so, until vegetables are soft. If the potatoes are large, they may need a little longer. If, when the vegetables are cooked, there seems to be rather a lot of liquid, turn the heat up and boil rapidly until reduced and syrupy.

## Jansson's Temptation

This is a completely and utterly unoriginal recipe, but I give no apologies whatsoever for including it. It is simply one of the most perfect, unfussy, yet wickedly rich and indulgent, potato dishes in the world. As if the crisp brown crust, and melting slow-cooked potatoes were not enough, there is also the salty tang of anchovies that have half dissolved into the cream.

If you are irrevocably convinced that you loathe anchovies, try the *Smoked Salmon Gratin* that follows and is very similar to this one, and almost as good.

---

900 g (2 lb) potatoes, peeled and very thinly sliced
2 onions, very thinly sliced
3 tins anchovy fillets

150 ml (¼ pint) single cream
freshly ground black pepper
150 ml (¼ pint) double cream

---

Grease 1 large or 2 smaller ovenproof dishes, about 5 cm (2 inches) deep. Arrange a layer of overlapping slices of potato on the base, then a layer of onion, and on this arrange a lattice of anchovies. Season well with pepper. Repeat layering, finishing with a layer of potato. Pour the oil from the anchovies and the single cream over the potatoes. Season with a little more pepper, and bake at 200°C (400°F) gas mark 6 for about an hour, until potatoes and onion are cooked. Cast an eye over it from time to time, to make sure it is not browning too fast. Pour over double cream, and serve.

# Smoked Salmon Gratin

This is a variation on *Jansson's Temptation* (see opposite). Most fishmongers sell off-cuts and scraps of smoked salmon at a greatly reduced price. They may be too bitty to serve on their own, but they are ideal for a dish like this.

Like *Jansson's Temptation*, this is a wickedly rich dish. Serve on its own, followed by a crisp green salad. Alternatively serve with plainly steamed vegetables.

A less rich version could be made using a good fish stock (see page 46) instead of the single cream, but let's face it, all that cream and melting potato is very tempting.

> **SUGGESTED MENU**
>
> *Smoked Salmon Gratin, Steamed Green Beans and Courgettes*
> *Orange Jellies*

175-450 g (6–8 oz) smoked salmon, sliced
900 g (2 lb) potatoes, peeled and thinly sliced
300 ml (1/2 pint) single cream
freshly ground pepper
150 ml (1/4 pint) double cream
lemon wedges to serve

Grease one immense shallow (about 5 cm – 2 inches deep) ovenproof dish, or a couple of smaller ones. Spread potato slices in overlapping layers on the base of the dish(es). Then add a thin layer of salmon, followed by a few twists of the pepper mill. Repeat until salmon and potato are used up, ending with a layer of potato. Pour over single cream, and bake for 50–60 minutes at 200°C (400°F) gas mark 6 until potato is cooked through and top is browned. If it seems to be browning too quickly, cover with foil. Pour over the double cream, and serve with the lemon wedges.

## Sautéed Potatoes with Green and Black Peppercorns

**SUGGESTED MENU**

*Grilled Pepper Salad with Olives and Eggs*

*Fennel Risotto, Sautéed Potatoes with Green and Black Peppercorns*

*Poached Pears with Strained Greek Yogurt*

Adjust the quantities of peppercorns to your own taste, and to fit the other food you are serving. A tablespoon each of green and black peppercorns give a pretty strong peppery bite. Halve the quantity and it won't be nearly as aggressive. Green peppercorns add an extra aromatic flavour and a bit more colour, though you could use just black peppercorns.

700 g (1½ lb) potatoes, peeled and quartered
10–15 ml (½–1 tablespoon) black peppercorns

10–15 ml (½–1 tablespoon) freeze-dried green peppercorns
25 g (1 oz) butter
15 ml (1 tablespoon) oil

**B**oil or steam potatoes until just cooked. Toss in a metal sieve to roughen up the surfaces. Crush the peppercorns coarsely. Heat the butter and oil together in a large frying pan, and add the potatoes and the crushed peppercorns. Sauté together until lightly browned.

### Other POTATO Recipes

**Hot Fennel and Potato Salad** *(page 97)*

# TOMATOES

We think of Italy as the home of the tomato. Travelling by train, one sees field after field dotted with red on either side of the tracks. They pop up everywhere in Italian recipes, on pasta, with meat and fish, in salads, and soups. It is hard to imagine an Italian meal bereft of tomato.

All too often, though, we end up buying greenhouse tomatoes, that bear little resemblance to fruit. They can be zapped up a notch with sugar, and the acidity of good vinegar, but never quite attain the marvellous flavour of a sun-ripened cousin. These need only salt, olive oil, and a few leaves of basil to turn them into a perfect tomato salad. Less exciting ones need the help of a fully-blown vinaigrette to make them worth eating.

Thin rings of sweet red onion not only look pretty, but also bring out more of the flavour. So too, do capers, thin strips of anchovies, and black olives. The classic Italian sliced mozzarella and tomato salad is always one of my favourites, sometimes with slices of avocado, or prosciutto, and always with lots of fresh basil, parsley or chives. Quartered hard-boiled hens' eggs, or tiny quails' eggs go well too. The French make what is sometimes known as a *hérisson* – hedgehog, out of this combination; a large tomato is sliced down vertically almost to the bottom, to form a fan. The hard-boiled eggs are sliced, and the slices wedged in the gaps of the tomato. The whole is decorated with dabs and dots of mayonnaise, topped with capers.

**Stuffed tomatoes** Tomatoes can be delicious stuffed. Slice the top off with a sharp knife, and carefully scoop out the insides. Season insides with salt, and leave upside down on a wire rack to drain. Fill with one of the risotto mixtures, and heat through to serve, or fill with cold cooked rice or pasta, mixed with seafood and mayonnaise. Or with capers, chopped fillets of anchovy, olives.

I love, too, the pretty red-jewelled effect given by minutely-diced, skinned and seeded tomatoes, scattered over a salad. It is the best raw way of using up a solitary tomato. You could add it to a tomato sauce made with canned tomatoes, in order to sooth a conscience ruffled by the use of tinned food, but there's little point. If the tomatoes you can buy are not that good, then tinned ones are usually better for cooking with.

To skin tomatoes for cooking or salads, cover with boiling water. Leave for 30 seconds, drain, and run under the hot tap. The skin should then pull away easily.

A tomato sauce is one of the most versatile of all sauces. Obviously, it goes well with pasta, but it is also the basis for tomato soup – liquidise with stock, or milk, add cream, chopped herbs, and some croûtons, and you're there. Ring the changes by adding orange juice, pesto, tiny pasta shapes, or rice, or by cooking finely diced vegetables in the soup, until just *al dente*.

Back with the original tomato sauce – cook meat or fish in it, with extra spices or herbs, such as lightly crushed coriander seeds, fennel, cumin, and a glass of wine. Again, the old familiars, capers and olives and anchovies, as well as courgettes, or red pepper, or green beans, can all leap in as well. Brown chicken breasts or fish steaks in the olive oil first. Set aside, and make the tomato sauce, returning the chicken or fish to the pan with the tomatoes, and any extra sliced vegetables.

Use a tomato sauce too, for vegetable gratins. Parboil vegetables – fennel, courgettes, celery, potato. Arrange in a layer in a large heatproof dish. Cover with tomato sauce, breadcrumbs, perhaps mixed with Parmesan, and trickle over a few spoonfuls of melted butter, or olive oil. Finish with half an hour in a hot oven.

One final gratin – the delicious Provençal courgette and tomato gratin. Slice courgettes and tomatoes thinly, and arrange in a gratin dish in overlapping layers like the shingles of a tiled roof. Sprinkle with Parmesan, pepper and olive oil, and bake in a medium oven until vegetables are cooked and browned.

## Basic Tomato Sauce

This is one of the most versatile of all sauces and most people will already have their own method for making it. I put this here simply for reference, and because it is the basis for many other sauces and dishes. For instance, liquidised and mixed with cream to go with the poussins below, or with ricotta for the tomato and ricotta soufflé. It is the basis, too, for a hundred and one pasta sauces (see page 22 for suggestions).

*Serves 2–3, with pasta*

15 ml (1 tablespoon) olive oil
or 25 g (1 oz) butter
1 onion, skinned and chopped
2 garlic cloves, skinned and
chopped
1 carrot, peeled and finely
chopped
1 stick of celery, cleaned and
finely chopped
400 g (14 oz) tin of tomatoes,
or 450 g (1 lb) fresh
tomatoes, skinned, and
roughly chopped

15 ml (1 tablespoon)
chopped, fresh basil, or
5 ml (1 teaspoon) dried
marjoram
15 ml (1 tablespoon) tomato
ketchup
salt and freshly ground black
pepper

Heat oil or butter in a pan, and cook onion and garlic until soft, without browning. Add carrot and celery to the pan, turning to coat in oil. Add tomatoes, herbs, tomato ketchup, salt and pepper. Simmer until thick and pulpy, with no trace of wateriness. Taste and adjust seasonings.

## Tomato and Chickpea Soup

SUGGESTED MENU

*Tomato and
Chickpea Soup
Brie Amandine
Orange Jellies*

This is a sturdy, stock-cupboard soup but none the worse for that. The freshness of the lemon juice gives it a sharp, refreshing vitality. It's an ideal winter soup, though that is no reason to ignore it completely on a damp summer's day. The spices and coriander give it a slightly Middle Eastern feel.

1 onion, skinned and sliced
3 garlic cloves, skinned and
finely chopped

15 ml (1 tablespoon) butter
2 x 400 g (14 oz) tins of
tomatoes

2 x 400-g (14-oz) tins of
  chickpeas, drained and
  rinsed
900 ml (1½ pints) chicken
  stock or water
1.25-2.5 ml (¼–½ teaspoon)
  cayenne pepper
1.25 ml (¼ teaspoon) ground
  cumin
1.25 ml (¼ teaspoon) ground
  fenugreek

10 ml (2 teaspoons) sugar
10 ml (2 teaspoons) tomato
  paste
salt
grated rind and juice of a
  lemon
chopped fresh coriander
  leaf, or parsley

Soften onion and garlic in butter. Add tomatoes with juice, and two-thirds of the chickpeas. Add stock, cayenne (take it easy at first) and other spices, sugar, tomato paste, and salt. Simmer together for 5 minutes. Allow to cool slightly and liquidise. Adjust seasonings and reheat with remaining chickpeas and lemon rind. Just before serving, remove from heat and add lemon juice to taste. Scatter with coriander or parsley.

## Tomato and Fennel Salad

This is really exactly as the title states – I sometimes add slices of mozzarella, or quartered eggs, and a few olives to flesh it out, but on the whole I find that the simple combination of fennel and tomato, lightly chilled, and served with lots of good bread to mop up juices, is enough on its own. Serve it as a first course, or with grilled fish or chicken, or after a tomato-less dish of pasta.

I rarely bother to skin tomatoes for a salad, but some people object to the presence of the skin.

SUGGESTED MENU

*Tomato and Fennel
Salad*
*Courgettes Paesana
in Bread Cases*
*Zabaglione Coffee*

| | |
|---|---|
| 3 heads of fennel | 2.5 ml (¹/₂ teaspoon) sugar |
| 3 large tomatoes (about 700 g (1¹/₂ lb) ), thinly sliced | 2.5 ml (¹/₂ teaspoon) French mustard |
| 15 ml (1 tablespoon) black peppercorns | 45–60 ml (3–4 tablespoons) light olive oil |
| 10 ml (2 teaspoons) sherry, or red wine, vinegar | fresh basil, chives, or parsley, chopped, to serve |

Cut stalks from fennel, saving a few of the feathery fronds. Discard damaged outer layer if necessary, then slice across very thinly. Arrange tomatoes and fennel slices on a large plate.

Crush the peppercorns roughly with the flat of a knife, or in a pestle and mortar. Mix well with the vinegar, sugar, mustard, and salt. Beat in olive oil to taste. Dribble dressing over tomatoes and fennel. Cover and chill. Serve sprinkled with fennel fronds and herbs.

## Tomato and Ricotta Soufflé

**SUGGESTED MENU**

*Tomato and Ricotta Soufflé*

*Pasta with Salsa Normanno*

*Elderflower Ice Cream*

This creamy, light soufflé uses as its base the simple tomato sauce given above, mixed with the pure and uncloying Italian cheese, ricotta. Always make sure that you buy it very fresh – most Italian delicatessens will have a daily supply. This soufflé will serve six as a first course, or two to three as a main course.

| | |
|---|---|
| double quantities of the Basic Tomato sauce (page 125) | salt and freshly ground black pepper |
| 100 g (4 oz) ricotta | 3 egg yolks |
| 15 ml (1 tablespoon) fresh basil, chopped, plus a few extra leaves for decoration | 4 egg whites |
| | 25 g (1 oz) freshly grated Parmesan |

Liquidise half the tomato sauce with the ricotta. You should end up with half a pint of thick purée. If not, top up with extra tomato sauce. Flavour with basil, salt and pepper.

Warm the sauce gently, and stir in the egg yolks. Whip egg whites until stiff, and fold into the ricotta mixture. Pour into 6 small ramekins, filling each one about two-thirds full. Sprinkle the tops with the Parmesan and bake at 200°C (400°F) gas mark 6 for 10–12 minutes.

Meanwhile, reheat remaining tomato sauce. Serve the soufflés as soon as they are ready, each decorated with a sprig of basil and hand the sauce round separately.

If you are serving as a main course, bake soufflé in a single 15 cm (6 inch) soufflé dish, for 22–25 minutes.

## Roast Poussins with Red and Green Sauces

Poussins, baby chickens, are quick to roast, and can be grilled too. They are moist and tender, but the flavour is a little bland, so season well. A slightly larger spring chicken has a better flavour, and will feed two.

Both the green and red sauces can be made in advance, and look bright and pretty, and yes, if needs be, Christmassy. Instead of using poussins, you could roast a whole chicken in the normal manner – season the insides, as well as the outside, with salt and pepper, and insert a whole onion in the cavity.

The green pea sauce, like the tomato sauce, goes well with pasta (add a little Parmesan), and can be served with fish, or with savoury soufflés, such as *Tomato and Ricotta Soufflé*.

SUGGESTED MENU

*Poisson Cru Niçois*

*Roast Poussins with Red and Green Sauces*

*Macédoine d'Ivoire*

Tomato Sauce:
**single quantity of the Basic
    Tomato Sauce (page 125)
150–300 ml (¹/₄–¹/₂ pint)
    whipping cream**

Green Pea Sauce:
**225 g (8 oz) frozen or fresh
    shelled peas
150 ml (¹/₄ pint) chicken
    stock, or water
salt and freshly ground black
    pepper
105 ml (7 tablespoons)
    soured cream, or creamed
    smetana**

**30 ml (2 tablespoons) single
    cream**

Poussins:
**6 x 450 g (1 lb) poussins, or
    3 or 4 spring chickens
    weighing about 700 g
    (1¹/₂ lbs)
15 g (¹/₂ oz) butter
salt and freshly ground black
    pepper
a few extra cooked peas
    (optional)
18 or so cherry tomatoes
    (optional)**

Liquidise the *Basic Tomato Sauce* until smooth, and stir in enough cream to give the consistency of thick double cream.

Next the pea sauce. Simmer the peas in stock or lightly salted water for a few minutes until just cooked. Liquidise peas with cooking water until smooth, and add creams. Season to taste.

Season the poussins inside and out with salt and pepper. Pop a whole cherry tomato inside each. Rub a walnut of butter into the skin of each and bake at 220°C (425°F) gas mark 7 for 30–45 minutes depending on size, until juices run clear. Baste occasionally with butter.

Reheat the sauces gently without boiling. Serve the poussins surrounded by a little of each sauce, a few extra cooked peas, and a few cherry tomatoes.

# CHOCOLATE

Cooking with chocolate is only worthwhile if you use the best. Of course, this is true of most things, but somehow it is easier to overlook when it comes to chocolate, surrounded as we are by a bombardment of cheap chocolate products. If you are going to make something as delicious and intense as say the chocolate ice cream given below, then your time and money will be wasted if you buy a cheap supermarket chocolate, or, God forbid, one of those ghastly blocks of chocolate-flavoured cake covering.

Use the bitterest chocolate you can find − if unsweetened bitter chocolate seems unobtainable, go for the best bittersweet or plain chocolate you can find.

The combination of chocolate and coffee is well known, and much appreciated by most people. Instead of serving pudding followed by coffee, make a pot of strong freshly-ground coffee, and pour over a bar of best chocolate, broken into pieces. Heat very gently, stirring until chocolate dissolves. Serve with whipped cream. If you are worried that some guests may prefer their coffee neat, then serve a bowl of broken pieces of chocolate and another of whipped cream, with the piping hot coffee, so that each can make their own choice.

On a hot summer's day, prepare double-strength coffee in advance and chill. Serve with a ball of the chocolate ice cream given below, floating in each glass − add whipped cream, a few nuts if you like, *et voilà*, a chocolatey version of Café Liegois.

**Chocolate and raspberries** This is a great combination, in particular try *Raspberry Coulis* with the chocolate ice cream, or with a gingerless version of the *Hot Chocolate Soufflé*. Make sure that the coulis is well chilled.

Alternatively, you could just serve plates of raspberries, piled on a bed of cream, with shavings or curls of chocolate scattered over the top. I must admit, though, that I always find shaving, grating and scraping elegant curls of chocolate, a slight problem. It's hard to prevent the chocolate beginning to soften in the warmth of one's hands. I suggest that you chill it well before you start, and dip your fingers in a bowl of iced water, before you begin.

One final suggestion, that involves no manipulation of sticky chocolate, and provides a dessert that can be put together over several weeks, as and when some delicacy catches the eye. Gather together a collection of nuts in shells, glacéed, candied and dried fruits, sugared almonds, and chocolate covered brazils. In Indian groceries you may find the beautiful large rough sugar candy crystals. Arrange separately on individual plates or bowls, and place in the centre of the table together with a bowl of pieces of superior plain chocolate, and superior white chocolate. Serve lots of coffee, and let people chat and nibble and sip, passing bowls around.

## Hot Chocolate and Orange Sauce

Here is a quick hot chocolate sauce, that is wonderful with vanilla ice cream – make your own, or buy a really high quality one made from cream and eggs and without additives, and this often disappointing restaurant dessert, is actually quite wonderful. It's lovely too with poached pears, the *Vanilla Soufflé* on page 180, or pancakes, nuts and whipped cream.

**SUGGESTED MENU**

*Grilled Pepper Salad with Olives and Hard Boiled Eggs*

*Fennel Risotto Sautéed Peppered Potatoes*

*Poached Pears with Hot Chocolate and Orange Sauce*

| | |
|---|---|
| 175 g (6 oz) plain chocolate, broken into pieces | 25 g (1 oz) caster sugar |
| juice and grated zest of 1 orange | 25 g (1 oz) butter |
| | 2 egg yolks |

Place chocolate pieces in a bowl, over simmering water, with the juice and zest of the orange, the sugar, the butter and two tablespoons of water. Stir, as chocolate melts, and once it is all happily amalgamated, leave it to get thoroughly hot, without actually boiling. Remove from the heat and beat in egg yolks. Serve quickly.

## Hot Chocolate and Ginger Soufflé

This is in several ways quite the opposite of my *Rich Chocolate Ice Cream* – it is hot, and light and fluffy, but still wicked and rich. But then, I suppose that that is the point of most chocolate puddings, and it is also the reason that most of us like them so much.

Before cooking this, read the blurb above the *Three Pepper Soufflé* on page 108. The quantities are not quite so copious here, so use either one wider soufflé dish, or a slightly smaller oval gratin dish. Other than that, the comments apply equally well.

**SUGGESTED MENU**

*Strawberry, Goat's Cheese and White Radish Salad*

*Pasta with Mussels and Orange*

*Hot Chocolate and Ginger Soufflé*

175 g (6 oz) plain chocolate, broken into pieces
3–4 bulbs of stem ginger
30 ml (2 tablespoons) syrup from the ginger jar
300 ml (¹/₂ pint) single cream
5 egg yolks
6 egg whites

Place chocolate pieces in a bowl with the syrup and the single cream. Place over a pan of simmering water, and stir until chocolate is melted. Leave to cool slightly.

Dice ginger, and stir into chocolate mixture, with the egg yolks. Whip the whites until stiff, and fold into the chocolate. Pour into an ovenproof dish, and bake at 200°C (400°F) gas mark 6 for 15–18 minutes (oval gratin dish), 20 minutes (soufflé dish). The centre should still be runny, but you might like to serve it with extra single or even double cream.

## Mexican Chocolate Sauce

**SUGGESTED MENU**

*Avocado Gratin*

*Roast Partridge with Mexican Chocolate Sauce*

*Steamed New Potatoes, French Beans*

*Raspberries with Bay Cream*

This is really just a jazzed-up tomato sauce. The chocolate, used as a seasoning, gives it a richer taste. The chilli gives it heat, though it could be left out to give a milder sauce. Serve this with turkey, chicken, grilled or roast, or cooked in the sauce for extra flavour. It does well, too, in its chilli-less form, with game birds.

1 onion, skinned and sliced
2 garlic cloves, skinned and finely chopped
25 ml (1¹/₂ tablespoons) olive oil
1 bay leaf
400 g (14 oz) tin tomatoes
50 g (2 oz) raisins
¹/₂ stick of cinnamon
150 ml (¹/₄ pint) dry white wine
25 g (1 oz) plain chocolate, broken into small pieces
¹/₂–1 green chilli (optional)
salt and freshly ground black pepper

**F**ry the onion, garlic and bay leaf together in oil until soft. Add tomatoes, raisins, cinnamon, chocolate, wine, chilli if using, pepper if not, and salt. Simmer together for 15 minutes. Fish out the cinnamon stick and bay leaf, and liquidise.

## Rich Chocolate Ice Cream

Italy's most famous ice cream is the black *Tartufo*, of the Tre Scalini café, in Rome. Every time I visit the Eternal City, I make a pilgrimage that is as important as any tour round the Vatican or Colosseum, to the remarkable Piazza Navona, once the site of Domitian's stadium, now the home of the Tre Scalini and its *Tartufo*. There is usually a long queue of Italians and tourists.

Why is it so good? Well, it's the blackest (*Tartufo* means truffle), chocolatiest, wickedest of ice creams, its interior studded with sticky glacé cherries, and best eaten with a large swirl of whipped cream – if you are going to be self-indulgent, you might as well go the whole way. Take the ice cream outside, and savour it as you gaze across the dramatic Bernini fountain of the Four Rivers, sprays of water glittering in the sun, or in the floodlights on a warm evening. Bliss.

I'm not claiming that with this recipe you can recreate the Tre Scalini *Tartufo* but it does share some of its attributes: it's very rich, and dark and indulgent. Below I've suggested several additions to the basic ice cream, though it is actually quite delicious on its own.

*Serves 8*

| | |
|---|---|
| 350 g (12 oz) plain chocolate, broken into squares | 2 egg yolks |
| 150 ml (¼ pint) milk | 300 ml (½ pint) double cream, whipped |
| 300 ml (½ pint) single cream | cocoa powder to serve |

SUGGESTED MENU

*Apple and Cannellini Bean Soup*

*Avocado and Peach Chicken Kebabs*

*Rice with lots of Herbs*

*Rich Chocolate Ice Cream*

**P**lace the chocolate pieces in a bowl over a pan of simmering water, with the milk and the single cream. Stir until chocolate melts, then whisk in egg yolks. Continue to stir until mixture thickens slightly. Remove from heat, pour into freezer container, and cool.

Turn your freezer to its coldest setting, and place chocolate mixture in it. When sides begin to set, fold into the centre. When the mixture is just set, but not yet hard, remove from the freezer, and beat hard. Fold in whipped cream, and return to freezer till solid.

Half an hour before serving, move from the freezer to the fridge. When ready to serve, scoop out spheres of the ice cream, and pile up on a serving dish. Dust with cocoa powder, and serve quickly.

**Additions** Fold any of the following into the mixture with the whipped cream.

100 g (4 oz) glacé cherries, halved; 4–5 bulbs of stem ginger, finely chopped; 100 g (4 oz) raisins soaked in a glass of brandy; 100 g (4 oz) hazelnuts, toasted on a baking tray in a hot oven, skins rubbed off, and roughly chopped.

# ELDERFLOWERS

There is a sturdy elder bush at the entrance to my block of flats. Throughout May I watch it carefully, monitoring the growth of the flowerheads, anticipating the first few dots of white and eventually the glorious creamy umbels. This, for me, is the beginning of summer. Of course, the arrival of the elderflowers doesn't guarantee sunshine for the next three months, but it does hold a promise of picnics and al fresco meals, of better days ahead, of a more invigorating way of life. Whether or not you believe in this promise depends on how cynical you are. Yes, we all know that summer weather is unreliable but there's no harm in imagining that this summer will be different.

For several years, I lived in an attic on the edge of Hampstead Heath, in London. A romantic scenario – I always felt that I should paint or write poems, but the great works never quite materialised. On warm June evenings, I went for rambles across the heath, returning in the twilight with a bunch of musky elderflowers. An hour or two later, a friend and I could be enjoying crisp elderflower fritters, or the sweet acidity of a green gooseberry and elderflower fool.

**Free flavouring**  The elder is an unprejudiced social leveller. It will grow in the south and the north, town and country, on the scruffiest piece of wasteland, or at the bottom of the best planned garden. It is there in abundance for everyone to enjoy, and is a delicious, free flavouring. For the few weeks of the year when the elderflowers are at their peak, make the most of their unique musky taste.

Search out an elder bush that is as far away as possible from the dust and pollution of busy roads. Choose flowers that are in full bloom, and shake off any clinging insects or debris. Never, ever wash elderflowers – water will rinse away the scent. If they are too dirty to use, then leave them where they are for passers-by to enjoy. Use them straight away – their scent fades rapidly once picked.

To make fritters, dip the flowers into a light batter. Fry head down in light oil, snipping off stalks close to the batter once it has begun to set. Turn over and fry other side until golden brown. Dust with sugar, and eat with a squeeze of lemon.

You can buy packets of dried elderflowers from many healthfood shops, and where they are to be used purely to perfume a dish, they make an adequate substitute for the fresh flower. Even so, I'm not terribly keen on their use. I like waiting for the first elderflower of summer, and I like the idea of that short season. For me the unique heady taste is enhanced by its association with sunshine and heat, and the pleasure of the first balmy days of summer. To eat elderflower ice cream in winter would be to rob it of its magic.

# Elderflower Syrups

It is worth putting aside quarter of an hour on two consecutive evenings in order to make one of the following syrups. They can be stored in a clean jar for up to a month in the fridge. Either could be used to dress a fruit salad, maybe with an extra slug of gin or vodka. Or fold a little into whipped cream to give a delicate muscat flavour – serve with fresh or lightly poached fruit.

They can also be used as hot or cold sauces with a plain vanilla ice cream. Pour a few spoonfuls over the ice cream, and serve with crisp almondy biscuits – again a dash of alcohol will turn this into a more sophisticated grown-up pudding.

When the weather is hot, use the lemony syrup to make a delicious cooling drink – dilute with fizzy mineral water or soda water, and if you like add a measure of gin or vodka.

## Plain Elderflower Syrup

---

3 heads of elderflower  300 ml (½ pint) water
75 g (3 oz) caster sugar

---

Place sugar and water in a pan over a medium heat. Stir until clear. Bring to the boil. Add elderflowers and boil hard for five minutes. Remove from heat, and leave to cool. Cover and leave in a cool place (but not quite as cool as the fridge) to infuse for 24 hours. Strain through a fine sieve or muslin, and bottle.

**Elderflower and Lemon Syrup**  As *Plain Elderflower Syrup*, adding the juice and finely grated zest of one lemon with the elderflowers.

## Elderflower Custard

**SUGGESTED MENU**

*Strawberry, Chinese
Leaf and Almond
Salad*

*Black-Burnt Fish
Steaks*

*Elderflower
Custards*

This is a rich and subtle baked custard. Serve it in small portions, with crisp biscuits. You might dress it up with a raspberry or redcurrant *Coulis* (see page 179), or serve it with the gooseberry sauce that accompanies *Elderflower Ice Cream*.

---

1 quantity Plain Elderflower
   Syrup
2 whole eggs and 2 yolks,
   beaten

300 ml (½ pint) whipping
   cream

---

In a large bowl beat syrup into the eggs and yolks. Bring the cream to the boil and remove from heat. Pour on to egg mixture, beating constantly. Strain to remove any threads of egg white. Pour into 1 large ovenproof dish, or 6–8 small ramekins. Stand in a roasting tray containing 2.5 cm (1 inch) of hot water.

Bake at 180°C (350°F) gas mark 4 for 45–50 minutes for a single large dish, 20–30 minutes for the smaller dishes, until custard is just set. Test by slipping a flat skewer into the centre of custard. If it emerges dry, or with just a very slight creaminess, then it is ready. Serve hot, or well chilled, and if you feel really decadent, spread a layer of clotted cream over the top of cold custards.

## Elderflower Ice Cream with Gooseberry Sauce

The creaminess of the ice cream is set off by the tart gooseberry sauce. As with the *Elderflower Custard*, you could add a soft fruit *Coulis* (see page 179), or serve it with any soft summer fruit or sweet eating gooseberries.

| Ice Cream: | Sauce: |
|---|---|
| **1 quantity Plain Elderflower Syrup** | **225 g (¹/₂ lb) gooseberries, topped and tailed** |
| **2 eggs** | **30 ml (2 tablespoons) water** |
| **300 ml (¹/₂ pint) whipping cream** | **sugar to taste** |

**SUGGESTED MENU**

*Elona Salad with Parma Ham*

*Tomato and Ricotta Soufflé*

*Ice Cream with Gooseberry Sauce*

**B**ring the syrup to the boil, and remove from the heat, pour on to the lightly beaten eggs, beating constantly, until you have a thick foam.

Whip cream and fold into egg mixture. Pour into a container and place in the freezer. When sides are set, fold into the middle, and return to the freezer. When mixture is thick, but not quite solid, beat hard to break any crystals. Return to the freezer to finish freezing.

Stew the gooseberries over a low heat with the water. Mash, and sieve. Sweeten to taste. Serve cold, with the ice cream.

## Elderflower Sorbet

This is a wonderfully cooling lemony sorbet – made for hot weather. It is the kind of pudding that is ideal to round off a delicious but filling meal with a touch of something slightly sweet and fragrantly scented on the tongue.

| **1¹/₂ quantities Elderflower and Lemon Syrup (page 139)** | **3 egg whites** |
|---|---|

**SUGGESTED MENU**

*Chicken Livers with Almond and Garlic Sauce*

*Aubergine Parmigiana with Porcini*

*Elderflower Sorbet*

**D**ilute syrup with 600 ml (1 pint) water. Pour into a container and place in the freezer. When edges are setting, fold into the centre, breaking up any crystals. Return to the freezer, until thick but not quite frozen. Beat well. Quickly beat egg whites until stiff, then beat in the sorbet spoonful by spoonful. Return to the freezer to finish freezing. Serve straight from the freezer.

## Gooseberry and Elderflower Fool

Gooseberry fool, a very English pudding, was the delight of late June and early July for me as a child. It takes me back to long summer lunches, out in the garden amongst the roses.

If, as occasionally happens, the gooseberry and elderflower seasons don't quite coincide as they should, flavour the fool with a tablespoon or two of elderflower syrup.

**SUGGESTED MENU**

*Parma Ham with Exotic Fruit*

*Fillets of Plaice Wrapped in Lettuce*

*Gooseberry and Elderflower Fool*

350 g (12 oz) gooseberries, topped and tailed
1 large or 2 small elderflower heads

40 g (1½ oz) butter or 30 ml (2 tablespoons) water
sugar to taste
300 ml (½ pint) whipping cream

Stew gooseberries with elderflower and butter or water until just soft. Remove elderflower, and mash gooseberries coarsely. Leave to cool, then sweeten to taste. Whip cream, and fold into gooseberries. Chill lightly.

My parents' garden stretches out far behind the house. There is a stream in a dip at the end,  well out of sight of the house, and hedges, a small abandoned and cracked swimming pool, the remains of an unused metal chicken coop half hidden at the bottom, and lots and lots of trees of many varieties.

The bushy dark green yew trees were always best for climbing and hiding in – one in particular became my den, a place where I could settle down comfortably in amongst the twisted branches. In one special place, they formed a natural armchair. I read there for hours. Eventually, in a fit of enthusiastic garden management, my father lopped some of those branches off – it was a long time before I forgave him completely.

There were many fruit trees too. The graceful medlar tree, with its trailing branches and little dark brown fruit, that made the most delicious jelly; acid crab apples; Victoria plums; a tall venerable pear tree; a peach tree (not the world's greatest success); and five or six varieties of apple tree.

The sturdy old cooking apple tree which put forth such a generous crop every year, was of great importance – not so much for culinary reasons, but rather because of the swing. My father, creator of this child's paradise of a garden, had strung it up for me, and on a blue-skied day, the pleasure of that rush up and up through the air towards the summer's leafy-green branches, mottled here and there with a glimpse of blue, a shaft of light, or the wintery bare lace of brown twigs, is still unparalleled.

I ate apples from the other trees, and cookers as well, savouring the challenge of the sharp juice. Some varieties were good, and some were better, but there was one uncontested favourite – the Beauty of Bath. Who could resist such a pretty name for a start? The apple itself was pretty too. When you bit in, it was sweet, and scented, and the white flesh turned not brown at the edges, but rose pink.

I tend to cook with eating apples, rather than cooking apples. Cooking apples like Bramleys dissolve quickly with heat to form a thick purée – ideal spiced up and seasoned, for apple sauces. But most eating apples have the advantage of holding their shape better if necessary, and being mashable, and I prefer their flavour in sweet dishes in particular.

For instance, you might stew a few Cox's, roughly chopped, core, skin and all, with a large knob of butter. When the apples are soft, sieve the whole lot, and sweeten. Add this purée to a *crème pâtissière* base to make a soufflé (see page 108), or mix with cream and eggs, add a teaspoon or two of orange-flower water maybe, and bake in a bain marie for a delicious apple custard. Or bake in a shortcrust case.

One form of the traditional French apple tart uses a thick apple purée as a base for the apple slices – line a tart tin with shortcrust pastry, and spread a thick layer of apple purée over the base. Top with concentric circles of thinly-sliced apple, dust with a little sugar, and bake until pastry is cooked, and apples are catching in the heat. Brush with an apricot glaze (heat apricot jam gently, then sieve, and dilute with a little water) *et voilà*.

I love that vast legion of apple pies and crumbles, with all their variations – but as recipes abound for these I shall just offer a small suggestion. Replace some of the flour in a crumble (up to a half), or a pie pastry (up to a third) with ground almonds, or rolled oats.

Caramelised apple slices make a delicious pudding too – fry apple slices in butter, sprinkled with plenty of sugar, and a pinch or two of cinnamon, until they begin to caramelise. You might flambé them too with brandy or Calvados, but either way, serve with lots of cream.

Similar fried apple slices, without the sugar, go well with meat and cheese dishes. Serve pork chops with fried apple slices and deglaze the pan with a little alcohol, and bubble through some double cream if you like.

Uncooked apples can be added to salads but don't over do them. A crisp Waldorf salad with walnuts can be lovely, or try combining shredded Chinese leaf, chicory, apples and walnuts, or toasted hazelnuts. Finally, though, it must be said that there is not much that can beat that simplest of combinations – a good apple and hunk of mature farmhouse Cheddar, or a piece of crumbly Wensleydale.

## Apple and Cannellini Bean Soup

**SUGGESTED MENU**

*Apple and
Cannellini Bean
Soup*

*Eggs Baked on a
Bed of Laverbread
and Orange*

*A Selection of
Dried and Candied
Fruits, Nuts and
little pieces of
Chocolate served
with Coffee*

The apples give this soup a gentle sweetness that is hard to define. It is rather a soothing and reassuring soup – no aggressive flavours, just subtle and velvety without being bland. It is wonderfully comforting on miserable winter days and refreshing in the summer too.

| | |
|---|---|
| 1½ onions, skinned and sliced | 5 ml (1 teaspoon) dried tarragon, or a large sprig of fresh tarragon |
| 40 g (1½ oz) butter | salt and freshly ground black pepper |
| 2 eating apples | |
| 1½ 400-g (14-oz) tins of cannellini beans, drained | 300 ml (½ pint) milk |
| | croûtons to serve |

Fry the onion until soft in butter without browning. Meanwhile, peel and core apples. Chop roughly and add to the onions. Continue to cook for 3 minutes, then add drained cannellini beans, tarragon, 450 ml (¾ pint) water, and salt and pepper. Bring to the boil and simmer for 5 minutes.

Cool slightly, and liquidise. Stir in milk. Taste and adjust seasonings. Reheat, and serve with croûtons.

## Calves' Liver Normande

If you can't get calves' liver, then use lambs' or even chicken livers for this recipe. As with all liver recipes, the really important thing is not to overcook it. As a child I loved liver, whilst contemporaries loathed it. It was, I suspect, because my mother understood that liver and leather need not be synonymous.

| | |
|---|---|
| 3 eating apples | 700 g (1½ lb) calves' liver, |
| 2 oz butter | sliced very thinly |
| ½ teaspoon ground | 3 tablespoons Calvados, or |
| cinnamon | brandy |
| 3 medium sized onions, | salt and pepper |
| skinned and sliced | |

**SUGGESTED MENU**

*Grilled Mussels*
*Calves' Liver*
*Normande*
*Pear Ice Cream in*
*a Chocolate Robe*

Quarter and core the apples, then cut each quarter into thirds, or halves if they are small. Fry apples in half the butter until golden brown. Sprinkle with cinnamon.

Meanwhile, melt remaining butter and sauté the onions until lightly browned. Add slices of liver, and sauté for about a minute until barely cooked. Arrange onions and liver on a serving dish, surrounded by apple slices, and keep warm. Deglaze the pan with the Calvados, and add 45 ml (3 tablespoons) of water, or chicken stock. Simmer together for 2 minutes, and season. Pour over the liver.

## Apple and Celeriac Salad

This is nothing more than embellishment and slight variation of the traditional French *céleri rémoulade*, celeriac in a creamy mustard dressing. Here I've used thick Greek yogurt, instead of *crème fraîche*, and have added a band of crisp apple, dressed in a simple French dressing – if you have any, use raspberry or sherry vinegar for this. The different textures and flavours are delightful. I find that a scented apple like the Cox's Orange Pippin makes the best companion to the celeriac. Serve it either as a first course on its own, or as part of a mixed hors d'oeurve, or with the main course.

**SUGGESTED MENU**

*Apple and Celeriac*
*Salad*
*Shellfish Stew (with*
*extra Mussels)*
*Rich Chocolate*
*Ice Cream*

1 very large celeriac root (or
two smaller ones)
60 ml (4 tablespoons) white
wine vinegar
3 crisp apples
15 ml (1 tablespoon) fresh
chopped parsley

Yogurt Dressing:
45 ml (3 tablespoons) Greek
strained yogurt
15 ml (1 tablespoon) French
mustard
5 ml (1 teaspoon) sugar

25 ml (1½ tablespoons) olive
oil
salt and freshly ground black
pepper

French Dressing:
15 ml (1 tablespoon) white
wine vinegar
2.5 ml (½ teaspoon) French
mustard
pinch of sugar
salt and freshly ground black
pepper
60 ml (4 tablespoons) olive
oil

Peel the celeriac and cut into julienne strips. As you work, dip the cut sides of the celeriac into a bowl of water acidulated with 30 ml (2 tablespoons) of white wine vinegar, to prevent discoloration. Bring a large pan of salted water, acidulated with the remaining 30 ml (2 tablespoons) of vinegar, to the boil, and blanch drained celeriac strips for 3 minutes. Drain and leave to cool for a few minutes.

Make yogurt dressing by beating all ingredients together well. Pour over warm celeriac, and turn to coat thoroughly.

Put all the French dressing ingredients into a screw-top jar. Close and shake well. Quarter and core the apples. Cut into thin slices and turn in the French dressing to season and prevent discoloration.

Pile the celeriac, with all its dressing, in a mound in the centre of a flat plate. Drain the apple slices, and arrange around the celeriac. Sprinkle with parsley, and serve.

# Apple and Pistachio Mousse

This is a delicate, pale mousse. Use the best apple juice you can find, or instead, stew 6 peeled and cored apples with the sugar and ground cloves, and a little water. Liquidise, and make up to 450 ml (3/4 pint) with water and Calvados.

Either set in individual glasses, or bowls, or in one large mould. You might make it 'rise' in imitation of a hot soufflé: wrap a long wide piece of greaseproof paper around the outside of an ordinary soufflé dish, so that this extends a good 12.5 cm (5 inches) above the top of the dish. Secure firmly with string.

Grease the inside of the paper with a tasteless oil. Pour mousse into 'collared' dish as normal and leave to set. Cut the string, and carefully peel the paper away. You will be left with a mousse that extends an inch or so above the rim of the dish.

*Serves 8*

**SUGGESTED MENU**

*Crudités with Goat's Cheese Sauce*

*Avocado and Peach Chicken Kebabs*

*Apple and Pistachio Mousse*

---

| | |
|---|---|
| 450 ml (3/4 pint) cloudy apple juice | 90 ml (6 tablespoons) hot water |
| 40 g (1 1/2 oz) caster sugar | 25 g (1 oz) shelled pistachios |
| pinch ground cloves | 300 ml (1/2 pint) whipping |
| 15 g (1/2 oz) (1 packet) gelatine | cream |
| | 3 egg whites |

---

Mix the apple juice with sugar and ground cloves. Sprinkle gelatine on the hot water in a small bowl. Stir until dissolved – if the liquid loses heat too quickly and the gelatine won't dissolve completely, heat gently over a pan of simmering water. Stir, and don't let it boil. Leave gelatine to cool until tepid and thick.

149

Whisk gelatine into apple juice – again, if you get lumps of gelatine, place bowl over a pan of simmering water and stir until gelatine is completely dissolved. Set aside to cool, until thick. Taste, and add extra sugar if necessary.

Chop pistachios roughly, saving a few to decorate. Whip cream, and fold into thickened apple juice with the chopped pistachios. Beat egg whites until stiff and fold in as well. Pour into mould, and leave in the fridge to set. Decorate with reserved pistachios.

### Other APPLE Recipes

**Brie Amandine** *(page 41)*

For years and years I pestered my father to plant a fig tree in the small garden of our cave in France. Unlike the other desires and wants of childhood, this

# FIGS

one quietly persisted. It was never desperate, never of immense importance, but it was always there, lingering at the back of my mind. And every spring and autumn when we returned to the village, my interest in the fig tree was revived. 'We could plant one, this year, maybe?' It became a family joke. My father insisted that it would take at least twelve years before we got any fruit, so it was hardly worth planting a tree. And then at last, when I was in my teens we reached the time when I could say with triumph 'See, if you had planted a fig tree when I first asked you to, we would be eating our own figs straight from the tree, right now'.

I still do hanker after a fig tree. I long to be able to wander outside, and pick half a dozen plump green or purple figs for lunch. The origins of this longing lay with an old and magnificent tree, that leant across a wall, into the courtyard of a friends house in Trôo. It wasn't his tree, but his neighbours were generous, and not always there. The courtyard was a suntrap, shaded here and there by buddleias, butterflies darting from bloom to bloom. I remember eating figs here, warm from the sun, picked not half an hour before. I must have been four, or maybe five.

Well, still no fig tree, and with no garden to my flat, the prospects seem dim. Instead I have to put up with buying figs from the market, sometimes bruised, or over-ripe, usually lacking the sweetness of a ripe Mediterranean fruit, usually expensive. But a trace of the voluptuousness remains, and every now and then one hits a sterling batch, with the sweetness and stickiness of honey.

151

**Accompaniments** By and large, bought figs tend not to be utter paragons of figgy attributes. They will need a nudge to give of their best. It may be as simple as the company of Parma ham, or crumbling moist Lancashire cheese. Halved figs, marinaded in orange juice, or brandy, or fruit-flavoured liqueurs, and sugar make a quick dessert. Or serve them surrounded by a pool of *Strawberry* or *Raspberry Coulis* (see page 179) with a swirl of sweetened whipped cream and a few toasted almonds, or hazelnuts. Some figs may need more attention – poach them in a sugar syrup with a cinnamon stick, or vanilla pod, and leave to cool in the juice. Try cooking them in the same manner as the *Peppered Pears* on page 171 – halve the amount of pepper and increase the sugar, and serve with *fromage frais* or Greek-style yogurt.

In the toe of Italy, households with their own fig tree dry the figs, stuffed with almonds, in the sun, and then in the oven. There is a tiny box of a shop near the foot of the dark twisting main street of Cosenza that sells only locally dried figs. Some are packed neatly in cartons, others wrapped in tight balls of vine leaves. The owner sends them to Calabrians living in foreign lands as a reminder of home and family. He swears that they are the best figs in the world.

Maybe. They certainly tasted good to me, though it was hard to tell back in rainy London, where the physical sensation of taste ended, and the romantic rose-tinted memories of that sun-drenched landscape of figs and poverty took over.

That's it. Enough of the reveries and the purple prose. Back to practicalities: bowls of unshelled nuts, fresh and dried fruits filling the centre of the table, often make a better finale to a winter's meal than a fiddly pudding. Linger over coffee with clementines, lychees, or hot house grapes, brazils, hazelnuts, walnuts, dried figs, muscat raisins, and dates. Like the Italians, stuff halved dried figs with nuts, or slivers of preserved stem ginger, and serve them on a bed of fresh bay leaves, or vine leaves if you are lucky enough to have some.

## Dried Fig and Orange Tart

If you are looking for an elegant twirl of a pudding, then this is not the recipe for you. This pudding is gooey and rich, and might even be described as a little childish. It is also exceedingly nice, and exceedingly popular. Few people seem to mind that the crushed digestive biscuit base lacks sophistication.

*Serves 8*

| | |
|---|---|
| 225 g (8 oz) digestive biscuits | juice of 2 oranges |
| 200 g (7 oz) butter | 2 eggs, beaten |
| 50 g (2 oz) sugar | 15 g (½ oz) pine kernels |
| 225 g (8 oz) dried figs | Greek-style yogurt to serve |

SUGGESTED MENU

*Warm Devilled Duck Salad*

*Fillets of Plaice Wrapped in Lettuce*

*Dried Fig and Orange Tart*

First crush the biscuits – place them in a clean plastic bag, and bash with a rolling pin, until reduced to crumbs. Melt 75 g (3 oz) of the butter, and stir into digestive biscuits with the sugar. Press down well on the base of the flan dish, and bake at 190°C (375°F) gas mark 5 for 5 minutes.

Meanwhile, chop figs roughly, and simmer with the orange juice for 5–10 minutes, stirring, until thick and pulpy. Off the heat, stir in remaining butter. When it is fully melted and incorporated, beat in eggs. Pour over biscuit base, and scatter with pine kernels. Bake for a further 17 minutes, until just set. Serve warm, with thick Greek-style yogurt, to cut the sweetness.

## Fichi Ripieni

**SUGGESTED MENU**

*Timbales de Courgettes with Salsa Cruda*

*Black-Burnt Fish Steaks*

*Fichi Ripieni*

Delicious figs filled with a mixture of ricotta and ginger. If you are serving them as a dessert after a fairly light meal, you will need two figs per person as below. But after a heftier meal, one fig per person will be ample – just halve the quantities.

225 g (8 oz) ricotta
25 g (1 oz) walnuts, finely chopped
5 bulbs stem ginger, finely chopped
15–25 ml (1–1½ tablespoons) syrup from the ginger jar

icing sugar to taste
12 figs
vine leaves for serving (an optional addition, for style alone)

Beat the ricotta with walnuts and ginger until smooth. Add syrup from the ginger jar – if you feel that the mixture should be a little sweeter, add icing sugar judiciously. Halve figs, and scoop out a generous teaspoon of flesh from each half. Beat into ricotta mixture. Fill each half generously with this mixture, and press together in pairs so that a band of pale purple pink links the two halves. Arrange on a bed of vine leaves. Serve chilled, dusted with extra icing sugar.

## Fichi di Sardegna

One summer several years ago, I stayed with friends in Sardinia. We were given a huge basket of plump sweet figs by a neighbour. That evening it seemed a pity to waste the embers of our barbeque, so we set about inventing a new Sardinian recipe – barbecued figs flambéed with a local liqueur.

**12 figs**
**50 g (2 oz) icing sugar**

**150 ml (¹/₄ pint) brandy**
**single cream to serve**

**H**eat the grill. Line the grill pan with foil. Thread the figs on to metal skewers, and grill, turning occasionally until the figs take on a glossy sheen. Remove from skewers and arrange in one large dish or smaller individual dishes, and sprinkle with icing sugar. Pour over any juices collected on foil. Warm the brandy in a small pan. Set alight and pour over figs. Serve flaming, with cream.

**SUGGESTED MENU**

*Poisson Cru
Niçois*

*Pepper and
Ricotta Parcels*

*Fichi di Sardegna*

# MANGOES

A friend who once lived in the tropics, tells me that there they eat mangoes in the bath. The fruit is plentiful and when warm and ripe from the tree, so full of sweet juice, that there is a logic to it. No need to worry about getting sticky, just let the tepid waters wash the trickle of juice away. After all, there is always another scented mango, waiting for you to bite into its soft flesh.

It sounds so idyllic . . . But now that imported mangoes have become so popular, we can at least buy them throughout most of the year, and aren't restricted to a short season. There are many varieties of mango – for cooking, for eating, for pickling, for keeping. The mangoes sold in our supermarkets and greengrocers are nearly all for immediate eating. If they are still hard, then keep them in a warm place for a day or two. If you are buying mangoes from an Indian shop, however, check what you are getting. Those meant for pickles aren't going to be much fun with Parma ham.

Eating mangoes, as they understand so well in the tropics, can be a messy business. If you wish to offer some at the end of a meal, then it would be thoughtful to prepare them beforehand. The easiest way, is to slice them downward, on either side of the narrow stone that runs from tip to tip. This gives you two thick ovals of orange flesh, and the stone still encircled by a band of flesh. Cut this band from the stone. If the mango is good and ripe, the skin will peel back easily.

Alternatively, and more elegantly, slice in towards the stone, as you might with a peach, and ease thin slices of mango away from the stone. The first few slices may be tricky, but it gets easier. When the mango is not quite at its peak, the flesh may cling more firmly to its stone. Serve the mango as it is, or macerate in lime or orange juice for a couple of hours. A slug of brandy, Cointreau, Midori or other melon liqueur would not go amiss, either.

**Fruit salad**  Pieces of mango, are, of course, delicious in a fruit salad. I prefer to keep the flavours simple and strong – the dark purple-black of grapes against the vivid orange looks superbly dramatic, for instance, as well as being a lovely coupling of tastes. Or thread a selection of three or four different fruits, cut into cubes if necessary, on to wooden kebab sticks. Serve as they are, or sprinkle with sugar (perhaps the cardamom sugar used in the *Mango and Cardamom Fool* here) or even with a twist of fresh pepper. They can also be lightly grilled – again sprinkle with sugar and maybe a little pepper, so that they caramelise under the heat.

In moderation, mango works well with savoury dishes. Try substituting mango for pear in the *Smoked Chicken and Pear Salad* on page 6. Or just use it on its own to make a small salad to accompany raw hams, or simply cooked chicken. Sprinkle with salt, freshly ground pepper, and add a squirt of lemon or lime juice.

## Parma Ham with Exotic Fruit

SUGGESTED MENU

*Parma Ham with Exotic Fruit*

*Spaghetti Carbonara con Porcini*

*Rich Chocolate Ice Cream*

If one could guarantee that every melon one bought would be a perfect specimen, then Parma ham with melon would be one of the most perfect ways to begin a meal. If you do get a good melon, then be generous – per person serve five or six (or more?) slices of ham, draped across one or two slices of melon, crescent tips pointing towards the sky, the way they do in many parts of Italy.

But if melons are out of season, or dubious, then try using some of the marvellous imported exotic fruits instead. Choose maybe three different kinds, and buy enough for everyone to have at least two pieces of each. For instance, one mango, two sharon fruit, and half a dozen lychees, would be just enough for six.

| | |
|---|---|
| A selection of ripe fruit, such as: mango, sharon fruit (or very ripe persimmons), guavas, papaya, mangosteens, rambutans, lychees, prickly pears. | 1 pomegranate (not absolutely necessary, but it does look very pretty) 3–6 slices of Parma ham per person freshly ground black pepper |

**P**repare the fruit. Leaving the skin on (unless it is very mottled), cut thin slices of mango. Slice sharon fruit. Peel guavas, and papaya, remove seeds and slice thinly. Score through the shells of mangosteens and rambutans, and remove inner flesh. Peel lychees.

Beware of the prickly pear. Don't, whatever you do, pick it up with your bare hands. The hair-like prickles are well-nigh invisible to the naked eye, but you'll be all too aware of their existence if they get stuck in your fingers. With a fork and sharp knife, slice off both ends of the fruit. Slash the skin from one end across to the other, and gently ease the skin away from the central core of the fruit. You should end up with a barrel-shaped piece of fruit, lying on a rectangular piece of skin. Move the fruit on to a plate and quickly discard the skin. Wipe down the chopping board thoroughly, and rinse cutlery under the tap. Then slice the skinned fruit.

Halve the pomegranate, and scoop out the seeds, discarding any of the yellow pith. Arrange all the ham, and all the fruit, except the pomegranate on one large, or individual plates. Sprinkle with lots of freshly ground pepper, and scatter pomegranate seeds on the top.

## Almond Roulade with Chicken and Mango

The following recipe sounds terribly complicated, but it is not really. Everything, except the roulade itself, can be prepared well in advance and then thrown together at the last minute. It does mean that you have to spend ten minutes or so in the kitchen between courses, but the final result is so impressive and delicious, that it seems a small price to pay.

| | |
|---|---|
| 4 large, or 5 small chicken breasts, skinned | salt |
| | freshly ground black pepper |
| 50 g (2 oz) butter | 2 mangoes |
| 60 ml (4 tablespoons) brandy | 175 g (6 oz) halved almonds |
| 300 ml (½ pint) double cream | 4 eggs |

SUGGESTED MENU

*An Antipasto of Salamis, Hams, thin Slices of Cheese and Olives*

*Almond Roulade with Mango and Chicken*

*Strawberry and Orange-Flower Sorbet*

**B**rown the chicken breasts in butter. Pour brandy and double cream into the pan and simmer for 10 minutes or so, until chicken breasts are just cooked through. Remove them from pan and tear into small strips. Boil the sauce hard until it is reduced by about a third. Add salt and pepper to taste.

Peel the mangoes, and cut the flesh from the stone. Cut half a dozen or so elegant slices from larger portions, and chop the remainder roughly. Set aside.

Spread the almonds out on a baking tray and toast in a hot oven, shaking occasionally, for about 10 minutes, until golden. Leave to cool, then grind two thirds to a rough powder.

Line a 33 x 23 cm (13 x 9 inch) Swiss roll tin with non-stick baking parchment. Whisk the eggs (with an electric beater if you have one) with a twist of salt and pepper until thick and foaming, then quickly fold in the ground almonds. Pour into prepared tin, and bake at 200°C (400°F) gas mark 6 for 8 minutes. Whilst cooking, clear a good area of your work surface, and on it lay a dampened clean tea towel. Cover with another sheet of non-stick baking parchment. As soon as roulade is cooked, turn out on to awaiting parchment. Quickly and carefully peel off the lining paper, and trim edges. Roll into a long loose roll, using the remaining layer of paper to prevent sticking.

Reheat sauce, reserving a couple of spoonfuls. Stir in chicken and chopped mango, and heat through thoroughly. Unwind roulade and spread with this mixture. Quickly re-roll, without the paper this time, lift gently on to a hot serving dish, and decorate with reserved sauce, almonds and mango slices. Serve quickly.

## Mango and Cardamom Fool

This is an intensely aromatic fruit fool, and very rich too, so it should be served in small quantities. You may find that there is enough to stretch to around eight people if necessary.

Save any left-over cardamom sugar to sprinkle over other soft fruit, or for later use. In the summer, use to make strawberry or raspberry fools.

**SUGGESTED MENU**

*Eggs Baked on a
Bed of Black
Salsify*

*Fillets of Plaice
Wrapped in
Lettuce*

*Iced Mango and
Cardamom Fool*

**6 cardamom pods**
**50 g (2 oz) sugar**
**2 mangoes**
**15 ml (1 tablespoon) orange-**
**flower water**

**300 ml (½ pint) double or**
**whipping cream**

**M**ake an incision in each cardamom pod and extract seeds. Grind these with the sugar until the consistency of icing sugar. Scoop mango flesh from skins and stones. Cut up roughly then mash with a fork. Stir in half of the cardamom sugar, and the orange-flower water. Whip the cream and fold into the mango purée. Taste and add more of the cardamom sugar if necessary. Chill lightly and serve with langues de chats or crisp wafer biscuits.

## Tropical Halva Cake

SUGGESTED MENU

*Timbales de
Courgettes with
Salsa Cruda*

*Grilled Chicken
with Anchovy and
Orange butter*

*Tropical Halva
Cake*

This delicious, gooey cake, filled with fruit, is best served
with lots of whipped cream, or thick, strained Greek
yogurt. If you're a vehement semolina-hater just try to
ignore the fact of its inclusion. The cake bears absolutely
no resemblance whatsoever, in taste or looks, to
semolina pudding, and I've known no-one who disliked
it . . . except for one person, who didn't like sweet things
at all.

*Serves 8*

50 g (2 oz) hunza apricots
   (available in wholefood
   shops)
1 mango
1 small pineapple
1 banana
75 g (3 oz) softened butter

75 g (3 oz) sugar
2 large eggs, beaten
pinch of salt
175 g (6 oz) semolina
10 ml (2 teaspoons) baking
   powder
60 ml (4 tablespoons) rum

Place apricots in a small pan and cover with water. Simmer
for 5–10 minutes until soft. Drain, reserving the cooking
water. Remove stones, and crack open to get at the almondy
kernels. Chop the flesh of the apricots, and the kernels.

Prepare the mango and pineapple over a bowl, to catch the
juice. Peel the mango, remove stone and dice. Peel
pineapple, and dice. Peel banana and slice. Toss all the fruit
together, with juices.

Line an 18-cm (7-inch) diameter cake tin with non-stick
baking parchment. Cream the butter with the sugar until light
and fluffy. Beat in eggs, and salt. Add the semolina and the
baking powder. Mix well, then fold in drained fruit. Pour the
mixture into the baking tin. Bake at 220°C (425°F) gas mark 7

for 10 minutes, then lower the heat to 180°C (350°F) gas mark 4 for a further 30 minutes until cake is golden brown.

Let the cake stand for a few minutes, then turn out on to a plate. Heat the rum with the reserved apricot juice, and any juices from the other fruit. Simmer together for 5 minutes, and then pour over the cake. Leave in a cool place until liquid is absorbed.

# ORANGES

I first smelled orange flowers when I was fourteen, in Famagusta, in Cyprus. On thinking about it, this seems strange – I'm sure I must have come into contact with orange trees before. But it must have been the first time that they had been in flower, as I can't imagine how I could possibly have forgotten my first experience of that most heavenly of perfumes.

I was on holiday with my parents. That evening I was feeling miffed. The handsome young waiter in the hotel had asked me to go for a walk with him, and my parents had refused to let me go. I can see now that it was a wise decision, but at the time I felt that young love had been thwarted. Bang went my first holiday romance, and I've never been much good at them since. Instead, I went grudgingly for a walk with my parents. It was dark, and the road only dimly lit. We were in the modern part of the town, squat, ugly, squalid houses lining the road. The night was balmy, with a gentle breeze, and all of a sudden, floating on the breeze came the magic of orange blossoms. The waiter was quite forgotten, and for a few minutes I was wholly entwined in that scent.

It's funny, isn't it . . . on that holiday we visited many of the great sites of ancient Greece – the Acropolis, Delphi, Epidaurus, Salamis – yet the only moment I can remember in detail is when I smelled the orange blossom in a dirty back street of Famagusta.

**Orange scent** From these delightful flowers is distilled orange-flower water, used with enthusiasm in the

Middle East to flavour sweetmeats, and also in Morocco to scent cooling salads. The dressing given below for an orange and mooli salad, is based on a recipe I glimpsed a few years ago in a heavy-weight Moroccan cookery book. It was written for the 'average Moroccan household'. I still have a photocopy of one of the recipes – it was for couscous with sheeps' heads. '*Cut the heads in half, but first shake well to dislodge the worms that nestle inside the throat and ears*' . . . ooh, it sends shivers down my spine. I've never tried that one. Another began '*Take 100 kilos of beef, or for a small household, 20 kilos will suffice*'. You then cut it into strips and dry it in the sun. I've never tried that one either.

I digress. Another interesting thing about oranges, is that a ripe one is not necessarily orange. The change in colour from green to orange comes only with a spell of cold weather. Oranges grown in the tropics remain green. So don't reject them out of hand – at least it shows that they haven't been dyed as many are. Some are coated in wax to prevent them drying out in transit and to give a longer shelf life. If you are going to use the whole orange, or the zest, it is probably wise to wash or even scrub it well first.

If you don't want the zest for immediate use, don't just throw it away. Using a vegetable parer, cut it from the orange in strips, backed by as little of the white pith as possible. Hang it up to dry in a sunny place, then use it as a spice for stews and fish soups. Bed a few pieces in a small jar of caster sugar for a few days, or longer, to add an orangey taste. Sprinkle it over fruit, or use to sweeten a plain junket, or a slow-baked, creamy rice pudding.

Fight shy of indiscriminate inclusion of orange segments in salads. Unless they play a major role, it tends to be a disaster, though not quite as awful as the addition of tinned mandarin pieces. But thinly sliced, with or without the peel, and dressed with vinaigrette, all they need is a few black olives and maybe a sprig or two of parsley, to make a refreshing salad. Instead of olives, you could add some thin rings of sweet red onion, or slices of tomato. For a sweet fruit salad, marinade slices with icing sugar and a teaspoon or two of orange-flower water, or a little more Cointreau, brandy, or other suitable liqueur.

## Moroccan Orange and Mooli Salad

SUGGESTED MENU

*Cauliflower and Cashew Nut Soup*

*Tandoori Chicken Kebabs*

*Moroccan Orange and Mooli Salad*

*Potted Stilton with Peppered Pears*

This is a cool, refreshing salad. Serve it either with plain grilled fish or chicken, or maybe better still, on its own, after the main course. If you can't get a large white mooli – a type of radish – then use cucumber instead.

1 mooli (white radish), peeled and thinly sliced
2 large oranges, washed and very thinly sliced
15 ml (1 tablespoon) lemon juice
10 ml (2 teaspoons) orange-flower water
10 ml (2 teaspoons) caster sugar
salt and freshly ground black pepper
45–60 ml (3–4 tablespoons) groundnut, or other light oil
15 ml (1 tablespoon) fresh parsley, finely chopped

Arrange mooli and orange in concentric circles on a large plate. Beat remaining ingredients together, and trickle over orange and mooli. Scatter with parsley, and serve chilled.

# Orange Butters

Flavoured butters are always a great standby, turning plain and simply cooked food into something rather more elevated, in one almost effortless stroke. Herbs or garlic, lemon rind and juice can all be beaten in, but I particularly like these two combinations. Either goes very well with grilled fish – try it with cod or hake or other firm-fleshed white fish, or grilled plaice or lemon sole. Add it too, to chicken breasts, grilled or baked in foil with a small knob of the butter, and a few carefully peeled orange segments. If you're pushed for time, then a disc or two will liven up plain boiled or steamed green beans, broccoli, leeks, courgettes, and other vegetables.

**Anchovy and Orange Butter**  More than enough for, say, 6 cod steaks.

5 anchovy fillets
100 g (4 oz) lightly salted
   butter, softened
finely grated rind of
   1 orange

juice of ½ orange
freshly ground black
   pepper

**SUGGESTED MENU**

*Timbales de Courgettes with Salsa Cruda*

*Grilled Cod with Anchovy and Orange butter*

*Apple and Pistachio Mousse*

Chop anchovy fillets very finely. Mash softened butter with chopped anchovy, grated orange rind and plenty of freshly ground black pepper. Add orange juice, and beat vigorously until amalgamated. Transfer flavoured butter to a sheet of greaseproof paper, and roll into a thick sausage shape. Rush it straight into the freezing compartment of the fridge, before the orange juice has a chance to seep out of the butter.

To serve, cut 0.5 cm (¼ inch) thick discs from the still frozen butter, and arrange on top of hot meat, fish, or vegetables.

### Olive and Orange Butter

50 g (2 oz) black olives,
  stoned and finely chopped
100 g (4 oz) lightly salted
  butter, softened

finely grated rind of 1 orange
juice of ½ orange
freshly ground black pepper

**M**ash the olives and butter together before adding the grated orange rind. Then beat in the orange juice, add pepper and transfer to the freezer as above. Serve in discs as above.

## Orange Jellies

SUGGESTED MENU

*Tomato and
Chickpea Soup
Brie Amandine
Orange Jellies*

Like many other people, I was put off jelly as a child by those awful school jellies packed with soggy tasteless tinned 'fruit cocktail'. But I've recovered, and discovered that jelly, per se, doesn't have to be disgusting. On the contrary, a cooling spoonful of real orange jelly, slips down a treat at the end of a large meal.

If you feel like being arty, then make layered jellies – make the first batch with Cointreau, and half fill glasses. Leave to set, then top up with a second batch, flavoured with Campari (which is very nice all on its own). For serious art, tilt the half-filled glasses and support with jam jars, or a box. Leave in a cool place so that the jelly sets at an angle in the glass. Then fill with the second jelly.

15 g (½ oz) (1 packet) gelatine
90 ml (5 tablespoons) very
  hot water
450 ml (¾ pint) orange juice,
  freshly squeezed

75 ml (5 tablespoons)
  Cointreau, or rum
sugar to taste
150 ml (¼ pint) single
  cream

**S**prinkle gelatine over hot water, and stir until completely dissolved. Cool until thick, but still tepid. Mix Cointreau with orange juice, and add sugar to taste. Beat 45 ml (3 tablespoons) into the gelatine, then whisk it all together. Divide between 6 glasses, and leave in the fridge to set – or in the freezer if you are in a hurry, but don't forget about it. Just before serving pour a layer of cream on to the surface of each jelly.

---

### Other ORANGE Recipes

**Pasta with Mussels and Orange** *(page 26)*

**Baked Eggs on Laverbread and Orange** *(page 31)*

**Duck with Marmalade Sauce** *(page 70)*

**Avocado and Orange Salad** *(page 78)*

**Strawberry and Orange-Flower Sorbet** *(page 184)*

**Dried Fig and Orange Tart** *(page 153)*

**Hot Chocolate and Orange Sauce** *(page 133)*

# PEARS

A truly good pear needs no embellishment, no mucking about, no clever little tricks. A perfectly ripe pear should be perfumed, and honeyed. Teeth should glide through the flesh, as though through softened butter, each bite melting in the mouth, with only a hint of a roughened texture. Such a pear is the equal, or even the superior, of all the newly imported exotica in our shops – the mangoes, the papayas, the lychees or the passion fruit.

And yet how often do we eat a pear that good? Unless you grow your own, and can pluck them from the tree at just the right moment, then it's a rare occurrence, accident, not design. By and large, the pears we can buy are green and underripe (or bruised and brownish and rotting – avoid these like the plague). They will ripen happily in the warmth of the kitchen, but the flavour will never match that of the home-grown fruit. When the area around the stalk begins to soften very slightly, then your pears should be ready. Most are at their best for only a very short period of time – a day, or in some cases just a few hours – though they can be kept for a little while longer, wrapped in paper in the vegetable tray of the fridge. And if you miss that day, then use them up post haste, before they begin to collapse, and are fit only for the dustbin.

**Pears and cheese** Like apples, pears go well with cheese – it's now a common enough combination. Crumbly Lancashire or Wensleydale are delicious but Stilton is the hot favourite, with considerable justification. Serve them together, untampered with, to finish a meal. Try the *Potted Stilton* recipe below, or make a pear and Stilton salad – slice pears thinly, toss in lemon juice, scatter with toasted almonds or hazelnuts, and serve with mayonnaise flavoured with Stilton or some other blue cheese. Laid out on a bed of watercress, you could present this at almost any stage of a meal – as a first course, with a main course of, say, cold meats, instead of a green salad, or instead of separate deliveries of cheese and fruit.

The simplest way to cook pears that are remaining stubbornly hard, is to poach them in a sugar syrup (see the *Raspberry Coulis* recipe on page 179) with a vanilla pod, or cinnamon stick and cloves, until soft. Add thinly sliced quinces, if you see any, or use diluted Crème de Cassis as a poaching liquid – a good way to use up the end of a bottle. Once the halved, or whole fruit are cooked, remove together with the vanilla pod or spices from the juices, which may need boiling down to a thicker syrup. Serve chilled, with thick Greek yogurt. Any leftover pears could be used to make a pear fool – liquidise pears with enough of the syrup to give a thick purée, and mix with equal quantities of whipped cream, or, once again, thick Greek yogurt.

## Potted Stilton with Peppered Pears

This is an extremely simple dish that can be prepared completely in advance, and it looks so elegant – ivory pears studded with peppercorns, and pale green cheese. I dreamed it up to deal with leftover Christmas Stilton, but it is so delicious that it's well worth going out and buying Stilton just to use in this recipe. If you wished, you could use port or brandy instead of sherry. Serve it either as a first course, or at the end of a meal, as a cross between a cheese course and a dessert.

| Potted Stilton: | Peppered Pears: |
|---|---|
| **225 g (8 oz) Stilton** | **3 pears** |
| **100 g (4 oz) unsalted butter, softened** | **150 ml (¼ pint) dry sherry** |
| **30 ml (2 tablespoons) dry sherry** | **7 ml (1 heaped teaspoon) green peppercorns** |
| **5 ml (1 teaspoon) green peppercorns** | **7 ml (1 heaped teaspoon) black peppercorns** |
| | **15 ml (1 tablespoon) sugar** |
| | **sprig of parsley to serve** |

Mash Stilton with softened butter and the sherry, until well blended. Pack into a small bowl, and make a criss-cross pattern on the top with a fork. Dot with green peppercorns. Chill.

Peel, core and halve pears, leaving stalks on where possible. Place quickly in a pan with sherry, and water to cover. Add green and black peppercorns, and sugar. Bring to the boil and simmer until pears are soft – a knife should slip effortlessly into the flesh. This may take as little as 5 minutes, if they are fairly ripe. Remove pears from pan using a slotted spoon. Boil remaining liquid hard, until reduced to about 90–100 ml (6 or 7 tablespoons). Pour over pears, and leave to cool. Chill.

To serve, slice each pear half thinly along its length, without cutting right through to the stalk end. Fan out one half on each plate, and pour 15 ml (a tablespoon) of the reduced cooking juices over it, together with a few peppercorns. Add a wedge of the potted Stilton, and a sprig of parsley.

# Macédoine d'Ivoire

A cool, perfumed, refreshing pale green and white fruit salad, the perfect finale to a summer meal. For extra emphasis, serve it in a plain glass or white china bowl. Or in the melon shell itself – rather than halving the melon, slice a lid off the top, and scoop the seeds out with a spoon. Scoop out flesh, taking great care not to pierce the walls. Fill with fruit salad just before serving – it won't all fit in, so keep half back to replenish the bowl.

**SUGGESTED MENU**

*Grilled Goat's Cheese with Harlequin Salad*

*Fricassee of Chicken with Lemon and Basil, with green Taglierini*

*Macédoine d'Ivoire*

| | |
|---|---|
| 3 ripe pears | 30–45 ml (2–3 tablespoons) |
| juice of 1 lemon | melon liqueur, or Poire |
| 1 green-fleshed melon – | William, or, at a pinch, |
| Ogen, or Galia | white rum |
| 350 g (12 oz) white grapes, | a small bunch of fresh mint |
| Muscat if available | caster sugar to taste |
| | white sugar crystals to serve |

Peel, core, and dice pears, tossing in lemon juice as you work, to prevent discoloration. Halve and remove seeds from melon. Dice, or use a melon-scoop to make little spheres. If you have time, peel and remove pips from grapes.

Toss fruit together with liqueur, and plenty of bruised mint leaves, saving a few to decorate. Taste, and add sugar if necessary. Chill, turning occasionally, so that all fruit is bathed in the juices. To serve, scatter with white sugar crystals, and decorate with reserved mint leaves.

## Pear Ice Cream in a Chocolate Robe

SUGGESTED MENU

*Grilled Mussels*
*Calves' Liver*
*Normande*
*Pear Ice Cream*
*in a Chocolate*
*Robe*

This simple pear ice cream would still taste quite exquisite without the chocolate coating, but the elegant contrast of dark and light, and of pears and chocolate makes the extra time spent well worthwhile. If you do have any syrup left over, don't throw it out – add chilled white wine, or champagne to make a very refined pear cocktail suitable for the smartest occasion.

100 g (4 oz) caster sugar
5 cm (2 inch) cinnamon stick
6 ripe pears
600 ml (1 pint) single cream

4 egg yolks
100 g (4 oz) plain chocolate,
broken into squares

Place the sugar and cinnamon stick in a small pan, with 300 ml (½ pint) water. Heat gently, stirring until clear. Simmer for 5 minutes. Peel, quarter and core pears, then halve the quarters. Simmer in the sugar syrup until soft. Leave to cool a little, then liquidise pears with two thirds of syrup.

Whisk cream into egg yolks, and stir over a low heat until it begins to thicken. Beat into pear purée. Taste, and add more syrup if necessary. Pour into a freezing container, and freeze until sides are firm. Take out of freezer and fold frozen parts into the centre. Return to freezer. When it is just beginning to set, beat well to give a smooth texture, and pour into a more decorative mould. Turn the freezer up, and leave ice cream to freeze hard.

Take the ice cream from freezer, and dunk the bowl for a matter of seconds in hot water. Turn out on to serving dish. Return to freezer for 15 minutes. Melt the chocolate in a small bowl over simmering water. With a spoon, trail the chocolate over the ice cream, to form a lacy outer coating. Put back in the freezer to set. Cover in foil. Move to fridge about half an hour before serving.

# Gratin of Fresh Pears

The beauty of this pudding is that the pears are barely cooked at all, just heated through, so that none of the fresh flavour is lost. The meringue is crisp on top, creamy underneath. It does mean, though, that you will need to use the ripest pears you can find. If necessary, you could poach very hard fruit in a sugar syrup – it shouldn't take long to do, but it does mean that what should be a fast, last-minute dessert, needs more forethought.

**SUGGESTED MENU**

*Iced Lemon Fennel Soup*

*Chicken Breasts en Croûte*

*Gratin of Fresh Pears*

| | |
|---|---|
| 6 scented pears | 3 egg whites |
| juice of 1 lemon | 175 g (6 oz) sugar |

Peel and core pears. Slice thinly and toss in lemon juice. Lay in a large heatproof dish. Whisk egg whites until stiff. Add half the sugar and whisk again until stiff and shiny. Fold in remaining sugar. Spread over pears, using a fork to swirl the surface. Quickly bake in a hot oven – 250°C (475°F) gas mark 9 – for 10 minutes until browned. Serve with chilled cream.

### Other PEAR Recipes
**Smoked Chicken and Pear Salad** *(page 61)*

# RASPBERRIES

Buying raspberries can be a tricky operation. I once had a huge row with a market stall-holder, because I insisted on checking underneath the top layer of raspberries in a punnet to make sure that at least some of the hidden fruit were in a consumable condition. As it happened, they weren't. All, except for the dozen or so on top were mouldy. This was true of most of the punnets on the stall. He banned me from his stall – small loss. But the queue behind me had shrunk considerably as I walked away, and I felt as if I had won a great victory for shoppers the world over.

To be fair, it is difficult to prevent a few raspberries from perishing along the route from plant to buyer. They are delicate, tender little things, after all. It is only fair to expect a few duff berries in amongst the good ones, and to spend a few minutes picking over them before using them in a recipe or serving them on their own.

The best raspberries have a short season, though there are some that fruit in the autumn. The simpler combinations are often the best. Raspberries with cream, flavoured like the *Bay Cream*, maybe, or sprinkled with sugar scented by having a twig of rosemary embedded in it. I particularly like them with cream cheese and *fromage frais*. Or place about ten raspberries in a glass, top with a layer of thick strained Greek yogurt, then with a layer of Demerara sugar, a second layer of yogurt, and finish with a crust of sugar. Leave in the fridge for an hour or two, and the sugar melts into the yogurt.

**Savoury raspberries** The use of raspberries in savoury dishes has become rather fashionable of late. Once in a while, this can be a great treat, though I think I would tire of it were it a daily occurrence. To make a raspberry vinaigrette, liquidise raspberries with olive oil, then sieve. Add salt, pepper, a pinch of sugar and lemon juice to make a vinaigrette, for avocado, say, or with less lemon juice to serve as a sauce, hot or cold, with grilled chicken, or thin slices of pork tenderloin. Substitute melted butter for the olive oil if you wish, or cream, or if you have any, a much reduced stock. Serve with a few reserved raspberries, and their leaves if you have them, for simple but effective decoration.

## Raspberries and Cream Cheese on Almond Tartlets

The crisp, slightly curved little almond biscuits, make pretty dishes for the cream cheese and raspberries, though they go well with many other fruits and puddings. You can substitute whipped or clotted cream, or thick strained Greek yogurt for the cream cheese mixture. You can eat the tartlets hot from the oven, or cold, but in this case don't fill them till the last minute so they stay crisp.

| The Tartlets: | The Cream Cheese Mixture: |
|---|---|
| 100 g (4 oz) butter plus extra for greasing | 225 g (8 oz) cream cheese |
| 100 g (4 oz) caster sugar | 25 g (1 oz) icing sugar |
| 100 g (4 oz) ground almonds | 2 eggs |
| | 350 g (12 oz) raspberries |

**SUGGESTED MENU**

*Medaillons of Avocado*

*Duck with Sweet and Sour Onions*

*Raspberries and Cream Cheese on Almond Tartlets*

Cream the butter with the sugar until soft and fluffy. Beat in the ground almonds. Place a heaped teaspoon of the mixture in each of the greased hollows of a tartlet tin. Bake at

180°C (350°F) gas mark 4 for 5–7 minutes, until lightly browned. Allow to cool for a couple of minutes, then remove from tins.

Beat the cream cheese with the sugar and the eggs. Pick over the raspberries, discarding any that are sub-standard. Fill each almond tartlet with a spoonful of cream cheese, and top with as many raspberries as will fit. Arrange on a large plate, so that everyone can help themselves. Scatter any leftover raspberries around the tartlets. Dust with a little extra icing sugar, and serve quickly before tartlets go soggy.

## Two Red Fruit Gratins

SUGGESTED MENU

*Cheese Mousse*
*Calves' Liver*
*Normande*
*Simple Red Fruit*
*Gratin*

Here are two very simple red fruit gratins – it's nice to use a mixture of fruit, but if your choice is limited, then use raspberries or strawberries on their own. You might like to add a handful of toasted almonds, for contrast.

One of the great advantages of these two recipes, is that if you feel exhausted by the time you reach the pudding course, or there is an enthralling conversation going on, you can just serve the ready-marinaded fruit, as they are, with whipped or clotted cream.

### The simple gratin:

225 g (8 oz) raspberries
225 g (8 oz) redcurrants
225 g (8 oz) strawberries
40 g (1½ oz) icing sugar

30 ml (2 tablespoons) Cointreau, gin, brandy, or other suitable alcohol

Throw out any duff fruit. Pull redcurrants from stalks, hull and halve strawberries. Mix fruit with 15 g (½ oz) icing sugar (or more if you think they need it), and the alcohol. Leave in a cool place, turning occasionally, for at least an hour.

Just before you are ready to serve, dredge with remaining icing sugar, and put under a very hot, pre-heated grill, until sugar caramelises. Serve immediately with whipped cream.

## The marginally more complicated version:

| | |
|---|---|
| fruit as above | 2 eggs |
| 30 ml (2 tablespoons) Cointreau, gin, brandy, or other suitable alcohol | 65 g (2½ oz) icing sugar 150 ml (¼ pint) double cream |

Prepare and marinade fruit as above. Beat sugar, eggs and cream together until smooth. Pour over fruit and bake at 200°C (400°F) gas mark 6, for 20–25 minutes until just set – it is better to undercook it than overcook, as it could go grainy. Serve hot or warm.

## Raspberry Coulis

This very simple fruit sauce turns many very simple puddings into something a bit more special. Pour it over ice cream, or serve it with fresh or lightly poached fruit. It goes particularly well with the *Vanilla Soufflé* below. It can be made with other soft fruit – strawberries or blackberries for instance.

### Made with fresh fruit:

| | |
|---|---|
| 225 g (8 oz) raspberries 15–25 g (½–1 oz) icing sugar | 15 ml (1 tablespoon) lemon juice |

Liquidise the raspberries with 10 g (½ oz) icing sugar and the lemon juice. Pass through a fine sieve, or a coarser one, lined with muslin, and add more sugar if necessary.

**Made with frozen fruit:** When raspberries are out of season, a reasonable fruit sauce can be made with frozen raspberries, and frozen blackcurrants also work well. I sometimes flavour this with a few lightly crushed peppercorns. The sugar syrup here can be made in advance, and in greater

179

quantity. It keeps well in the fridge and can be used for poaching pears, peaches, bananas and other fruit.

---

| | |
|---|---|
| **100 g (4 oz) caster sugar** | **225 g (8 oz) frozen** |
| **150 ml (¼ pint) water** | **raspberries or** |
| | **blackcurrants** |

---

**F**irst make a sugar syrup. Place sugar and water in a pan, and bring gently to the boil, stirring until sugar dissolves completely and syrup is clear. Simmer for 3 minutes.

Add the frozen fruit, and simmer for a further 5 minutes, until fruit is soft. Pass it through a fine sieve, or a coarser one, lined with muslin to get rid of the pips.

## Vanilla Soufflé

SUGGESTED MENU

*Crudités with Pesto and Tofu Sauce*

*Pasta with Mussels and Orange*

*Green Salad*

*Vanilla Soufflé with Raspberry Coulis*

This is delicious, and rather pretty served with a raspberry coulis. Its base, the thick egg and milk custard thickened with flour, is a *crème pâtissière*, that could also be used to spread on the base of a pastry case and topped with fruit to make a French-style fruit tart.

And you could turn the whole thing into a raspberry soufflé by stirring the fresh raspberry coulis into half of the *crème pâtissière*, and using that as a base for the soufflé.

---

| | |
|---|---|
| **450 ml (¾ pint) milk** | **75 g (3 oz) caster sugar** |
| **1 vanilla pod** | **40 g (1½ oz) flour** |
| **5 egg yolks** | **6 egg whites** |

---

**P**ut the milk and vanilla pod in a pan, and bring gently to the boil. Turn the heat down to its lowest setting, and leave for 15 minutes to infuse. Remove the vanilla pod.

Beat the egg yolks with the sugar until pale and fluffy. Stir in the flour, and whisk in the hot milk. Return mixture to the pan, and bring slowly to the boil, stirring constantly. Simmer for 2 minutes, and beat well off the heat to smooth out any lumps. Cool until tepid.

Whisk the egg whites until stiff, and fold into the custard mixture. Pour into a soufflé dish, and bake at 200°C (400°F) gas mark 6 for 22–25 minutes. Serve quickly with the *Raspberry Coulis*.

## Raspberries with Bay Cream

If you keep a fresh bay leaf in a small jar of caster sugar for a week, you will end up with the most beautifully scented sugar, that goes particularly well with raspberries. Just sprinkle over, or use to sweeten whipped cream. If, however, such forethought was lacking, try flavouring cream this way. The almond tartlets from the recipe on page 177 go very well.

SUGGESTED MENU

*Avocado Gratin*

*Roast Partridge with Mexican Chocolate Sauce*

*Steamed New Potatoes*

*Raspberries with Bay Cream*

---

**300 ml (¹/₂ pint) double cream**
**1 bay leaf, plus a dozen or more fresh leaves for decoration**

**15 g (¹/₂ oz) caster sugar**
**700 g (1¹/₂ lbs) raspberries**

---

Place the cream, with the bay leaf and the sugar in a small pan. Stir, then bring gently to the boil. Taste, and add a little extra sugar if the raspberries are not too sweet. Turn the heat down low, cover and leave to infuse for 10 minutes. Leave to cool.

Pick over the raspberries, discarding any duff ones. Either pile up the raspberries on a bed of bay leaves on a large plate, and pass bay cream around separately, or divide raspberries between 6 plates or bowls, pour a little bay cream over each, and decorate with a couple of bay leaves.

# STRAWBERRIES

When I was young, we often used to go on family outings to the many auction sales in the countryside around the village where we lived, in France. They were gay, happy occasions, and whole families, like us, would treat them as a day out. In the morning they would view the lots, then trot off for a picnic lunch, and return later for the sale itself.

On one such occasion, my parents lost me as they were returning from their lunch. Anxiously rounding a bend in the lane, they saw ahead of them a huge French family, grandparents, parents, children and cousins, seated around a long trestle table and tucking into the final part of their midday meal. And somehow, in the five minutes that had elapsed, I had inveigled my way into a position at the head of the table. I too, was enjoying the magnificent strawberry tart.

**Strawberry tarts**  I don't remember this occasion at all, but I do remember other such tarts, a focal point in every *pâtissier's* window, and many festivities. They are not difficult to make – fill a blind-baked shortcrust case with *crème pâtissière* (page 180) and then cover with concentric circles of hulled and halved strawberries. Finish with a redcurrant (or quince) glaze made by heating one tablespoon of redcurrant jelly with two teaspoons of water. If you come across any tiny wild wood strawberries, eke them out by using them in this kind of tart for a very special dessert.

Strawberries can be used instead of raspberries in many recipes – they are included in both the *Red Fruit Gratin* recipes (page 178), and substituted for raspberries in the other recipes in that chapter.

When you get the perfect, but rather rare, sweet and scented strawberries, the kind that instantly tell you that strawberries are your favourite fruit, don't play around with them too much. Strawberries and cream is unbeatable, or halved strawberries on a bed of *Raspberry Coulis*. A few twists of the peppermill over the fruit, and a squeeze of lemon juice, is an unusual, but delicious way of bringing out their full flavour.

As an extension of this, make a simple salad to go with Parma ham, or smoked chicken, by dressing hulled halved strawberries with a peppery vinaigrette, and adding a few leaves of fresh mint. To make an Elona Salad, add thin slices of cucumber, first sprinkled with salt and a little wine vinegar, drained in a colander for an hour, then rinsed and dried.

## Strawberry, Goat's Cheese and White Radish Salad

This is a very delicious summery salad, that should be served on its own as a first course. If you can't get a white radish (mooli), use cucumber instead, prepared as for an Elona Salad (see introduction to this chapter). Prepare all the components in advance, and combine at the last minute.

| | |
|---|---|
| 15 ml (1 tablespoon) lemon juice | 1 medium white radish, peeled and sliced |
| 45 ml (3 tablespoons) light olive oil | 225 g (8 oz) strawberries, hulled and halved |
| salt, freshly ground black pepper | 1 small goat's cheese, or a 2.5 cm (1 inch) slice of |
| pinch of sugar | goat's cheese log |
| | basil |

**SUGGESTED MENU**

*Strawberry, Goat's Cheese and White Radish Salad*

*Pasta with Mussels and Orange*

*Hot Chocolate and Ginger Soufflé*

ut lemon juice, olive oil, salt, pepper and sugar into a
screw-top jar, close, and shake well.

Toss the radish slices and strawberries separately in
dressing. Arrange on a large plate. Cut rind off cheese, and
crumble or dice finely. Sprinkle over the radish and
strawberries. Scatter roughly chopped basil over the top, and
serve lightly chilled.

## Strawberry and Orange-Flower Sorbet

SUGGESTED MENU

*Crudités with
Goat's Cheese
Sauce*

*Fennel Siciliano*

*Strawberry and
Orange-Flower
Sorbet*

Sorbets are always cool and refreshing, and are a perfect
way to finish a summer meal. As an extra you might add a
*Raspberry* or *Strawberry Coulis* (page 179), or a little gin.
You could accompany this sorbet with the *Almond Tartlets*
on page 177.

---

**350 g (12 oz) strawberries,
  hulled**
**50 g (2 oz) icing sugar**
**juice and finely grated zest
  of 1 orange**

**150 g (6 oz) caster sugar**
**10 ml (2 teaspoons) orange-
  flower water**

---

iquidise strawberries with icing sugar and orange juice,
then sieve. Add the grated orange zest.

Put the caster sugar, and 450 ml (³/₄ pint) water in a pan.
Bring to the boil, stirring until clear. Simmer for 5 minutes.
Cool. Add to the strawberries. Add the orange-flower water.
Taste, and add more orange-flower water, or sugar, if
necessary.

Pour into a container, and leave in the freezer until sides
are beginning to set. Fold the edges into the middle, breaking
up any ice crystals. Return to the freezer. When the ice is on
the verge of hardening, take out and beat vigorously, then put
back in the freezer to finish freezing.

## Strawberry, Chinese Leaf and Almond Salad

Like the preceding salad, serve this as a first course, or as a mid-meal refresher. A few pieces of smoked chicken could be added to flesh it out, and so turn it into the focal point of the meal.

**SUGGESTED MENU**

*Strawberry, Chinese Leaf and Almond Salad*

*Tortellini with Cream, Mint and Lemon Sauce*

*Green Salad served with Cheese and Water Biscuits*

10 ml (2 teaspoons) white wine vinegar
45 ml (3 tablespoons) olive oil
salt and freshly ground pepper
pinch of sugar

25 g (1 oz) flaked almonds
1/2 a head of Chinese leaf, shredded
225 g (8 oz) strawberries, hulled and halved
roughly chopped chives

Put vinegar, olive oil, salt, pepper and sugar into a screw-top jar, close and shake well.

Spread almonds out on a baking sheet, and put in a hot oven for 5–10 minutes, until lightly browned. Leave to cool.

Spread Chinese leaf out on a large plate, arrange strawberries on top, then scatter with almonds. Dribble dressing over the salad, and finish with a sprinkling of chives. Serve lightly chilled.

## Chocolate and Cointreau-Coated Strawberries

These must be made on the day they are to be eaten and preferably within a few hours of the meal. Left around for too long, the strawberry juice begins to seep out, while the fruit quickly softens. If you had time, you could make

**SUGGESTED MENU**

*Iced Lemon
Fennel Soup*

*Chicken Breasts
en Croûte*

*Chocolate and
Cointreau-Coated
Strawberries*

several different varieties – omit the alcohol in some, use milk or white chocolate in others. Be careful not to overheat white chocolate though.

| | |
|---|---|
| 225 g (8 oz) plain chocolate, broken into pieces | 30 ml (2 tablespoons) Cointreau or brandy |
| 50 g (2 oz) butter | 225–350 g (8–12 oz) strawberries |

Place chocolate pieces in a bowl with the butter and Cointreau. Place over a pan of simmering water, stirring occasionally, until chocolate is melted and well mixed with other ingredients. Turn the heat under the pan down low.

Line a baking tray with a sheet of greaseproof paper, and oil lightly. One by one, pick up the strawberries by their green leaves, and dip them into the chocolate, covering about two-thirds of each fruit. Leave to set on the greaseproof paper.

**Other STRAWBERRY Recipes**

**Raspberry Coulis** *(page 179)*
**Red Fruit Gratin** *(page 178)*

# INDEX

If you have enjoyed this book, you may be interested in other titles in this series, also published by Ebury Press:

**The Essential Mosimann**  *Anton Mosimann*  £9.99

**Roast Chicken & Other Stories**  *Simon Hopkinson*  £10.99
(winner of both the André Simon Memorial Fund Book Award 1994 and the Glenfiddich Food and Drink Award 1995)

---

Available from good book shops or simply telephone Murlyn Services on 01279 427203.

Postage and packing are free.

You may pay by cheque/postal order/credit card and should allow 28 days for delivery.